Hannah Arendt

ALSO BY ANNE C. HELLER

Ayn Rand and the World She Made

Hannah Arendt

A LIFE IN
DARK TIMES

ANNE C. HELLER

ICONS SERIES

New Harvest
Houghton Mifflin Harcourt
BOSTON • NEW YORK
2015

This edition published by special arrangement with Amazon Publishing

For information about permission to reproduce selections
from this book, go to www.apub.com.

www.hmhco.com

Library of Congress Cataloging-in-Publication Data is available.
ISBN 978-0-544-45619-8

Book design by Brian Moore

Printed in the United States of America
DOC 10 9 8 7 6 5 4 3 2 1

For David H. de Weese

Contents

Indeed I live in the dark ages!
A guileless word is an absurdity. A smooth forehead betokens
A hard heart. He who laughs
Has not yet heard
The terrible tidings.

— BERTOLD BRECHT, "To Posterity," cited in the
introduction to *Men in Dark Times* by Hannah Arendt[1]

I

Eichmann in Jerusalem

1961–1963

> Going along with the rest and wanting to say "we" were
> quite enough to make the greatest of all crimes possible.
> — HANNAH ARENDT, interview with Joachim Fest, 1964.[1]

A FTERWARD, WHEN HANNAH Arendt published her book-length account of the trial of Adolf Eichmann, the fugitive Nazi SS officer who had helped to implement Adolf Hitler's Final Solution, the tumult the book created deeply shocked her. "People are resorting to any means to destroy my reputation," she wrote to her friend Karl Jaspers soon after the book, *Eichmann in Jerusalem: A Report on the Banality of Evil,* appeared in 1963. "They have spent weeks trying to find something in my past that they can hang on me."[2] The Anti-Defamation League and other Jewish organizations, the editors of influential magazines she had written for, faculty members at colleges where she earned a precarious living as a visiting professor, and friends from every period of her life objected to her characterization of Eichmann, who had been popularly branded "the most evil monster of humanity,"[3] as "terribly and terrifyingly normal."[4] Many were infuriated by her depiction of Nazi-era European Jewish leaders — some of whom were still alive and highly regarded — as having ("almost without ex-

ception")[5] cooperated with Eichmann in sending ordinary Jews
to Auschwitz, Treblinka, and Chelmno. Where only months
earlier Arendt had been celebrated as a brilliant, original, and
deeply humanistic political thinker, she was now attacked as arrogant, ill-informed, heartless, a dupe of Eichmann, an enemy
of Israel, and a "self-hating Jewess."[6] "What a risky business to
tell the truth on a factual level without theoretical and scholarly embroidery," she wrote to her best friend and steadfast de-
fender Mary McCarthy.[7] But the trouble with her book *was* its
theory—namely, that ordinary men and women, driven not by
personal hatred or by extreme ideology but merely by middle-
class ambitions and an inability to empathize, voluntarily ran
the machinery of the Nazi death factories, and that the victims,
when pushed, would lie to themselves and comply. The book
launched a pitched battle among intellectuals in the United
States. It blunted Arendt's reputation at its height and has cast a
shadow on her legend ever since.

Hannah Arendt was seated in the press benches when the
Eichmann trial opened to a tidal wave of publicity on April 11,
1961, in a makeshift courtroom in west Jerusalem. The State of
Israel was only thirteen years old.[8] No Israeli courthouse was big
enough to accommodate the spectacle, so a brand-new perfor-
mance theater called the House of the People was taken over for
the proceedings. It seated 750 people, but interest far outpaced
capacity. In the opening days, as many as seven hundred reporters from three dozen countries, international politicians and ce-
lebrities, jurists, Israeli and European camp survivors, historians,
and tourists competed to squeeze into the arena for a glimpse
of the notorious Nazi.[9] Arendt was on assignment for *The New
Yorker,* and on many days she brought along her seventeen-
year-old first cousin once removed, Edna Brocke, née Fuerst,
who had grown up in Israel. Taking notes nearby were former
war correspondent Martha Gellhorn, representing the *Atlantic
Monthly*; Elie Wiesel, writing for the Yiddish-language Ameri-

can *Jewish Daily Forward*; former deputy judge advocate general Lord Russell of Liverpool and Oxford professor Hugh Trevor-Roper, both writing for the *London Sunday Times*; along with reporters from the *New York Times, Der Spiegel,* and the *Washington Post.*[10] Cables and electrical wires crisscrossed the courtroom floor[11] to transmit the first continuous live television feed and videotaping of a judicial proceeding for an international audience,[12] and transcripts were distributed daily. Later, Arendt's critics would claim that she attended too few courtroom sessions and depended too heavily on tapes and transcripts, and in fact she was on hand in Jerusalem for a total of only five or six weeks of the five-month trial. But others also came and went, while the world watched on television.

The indictment against Eichmann was read by the chief judge on the first day of the trial; it ran to fifteen counts. These enumerated "crimes against the Jewish people" and "against humanity" that had been committed or caused by Eichmann between 1938 and 1945, beginning with his alleged participation in the murderous Kristallnacht pogroms of November 1938 and encompassing the forced transportation and extermination of the majority of Jews then living in Germany, the Axis countries, and the nations occupied by the German army during the war years. The indictment listed the concentration and death camps to which Eichmann "and others" knowingly sent Jews for the purpose of mass murder, the approximate number of Jews sent to the camps, and the dates during which the camps operated.[13] At the end of the reading, Eichmann, asked if he understood the indictment, spoke for the first time. "Yes, certainly," he said in German. Asked how he pleaded, he answered, "Not guilty in the sense of the indictment."

There were a number of reasons for the almost hysterical interest in the Eichmann trial — the international equivalent of the O. J. Simpson trial in its day. At the end of World War II, hundreds of fugitive Nazi officers were rumored to be hiding in towns and cities around the world, evil phantoms abetted by right-wing governments and networks of fascist fellow travelers. Eichmann and his bosses in the notorious SS, or Schutzstaffel — Heinrich Himmler's elite paramilitary corps, which was directly responsible for carrying out Hitler's plan to exterminate the entire Jewish population of Europe — had either disappeared, been murdered, or, in the case of Himmler, committed suicide[14] and thus escaped prosecution and sentencing during the historic war crimes trials at Nuremberg in 1945 and 1946. Partly as a result, the destruction of as many as six million Jewish men, women, and children — murder on a scale previously unknown in history — had not been thoroughly adjudicated or even acknowledged at Nuremberg or in the successor tribunals of the late 1940s, which had focused on Germany's illegal actions against other sovereign states in Europe. With Eichmann now in the seat of judgment in Jerusalem, the full story of the Jewish Holocaust, including, for the first time, the testimony of concentration camp survivors, would finally be heard. Or so the young State of Israel expected.

Another reason was that a year earlier, in May 1960, Israeli secret service agents had extracted Eichmann from his hiding place in Argentina, sedated him, kidnapped him, and brought him to Jerusalem in a dramatic, extralegal maneuver that had been cheered, criticized, and generally debated around the world for months before the trial.

The compelling attraction for most observers and for Arendt, however, was the mysterious figure of Eichmann himself, who, for his own protection, sat sealed in a bulletproof glass cage at the foot of the judges' raised platform for the duration of the trial. Slight, balding, bespectacled, with a runny nose and a compulsive twist of his thin and bitter mouth, he looked more like "a ghost who has a cold on top of that," as Arendt aptly described him in a letter to Karl Jaspers,[15] than the representative of a self-appointed master race. He had been the head of the Office of Jewish Affairs of the Gestapo, the Nazi secret police, as well as a midranking lieutenant colonel in Himmler's murderous SS, and he was considered the most wanted war criminal alive in the early 1960s. The Israeli and American newspapers of the period characterized him not only as monstrous and "bloodthirsty" but also as Hitler's foremost architect of and technician for the implementation of "the Final Solution to the Jewish Question," a particularly repellent Nazi euphemism for unprecedented genocide.[16] This last characterization of Eichmann turned out not to be entirely credible, as Arendt and others made clear at the time.

Everyone agreed at the outset that Eichmann was a strangely anemic-appearing exemplar of demonic evil. A high school dropout and a failed traveling "vacuum-oil" salesman, he was "the *déclassé* son of a solid middle-class family," Arendt recorded in *Eichmann in Jerusalem,* although a German historian named Bettina Stangneth has recently cast doubt on his black sheep status and painted his whole family in a darker light. He told Israeli interrogators that he had joined the Nazi Party in 1932, a year before Hitler seized power, for no particular reason except that a party official who was also a socially prominent family friend had suggested it. Soon thereafter, he was fired from his sales job, and the friend, one Ernst Kaltenbrunner, offered him a paid position in the elite SS corps of the Reich security police. By Eichmann's own account, in the following years he discovered in himself a gift for navigating large bureaucracies and orchestrating complex administrative tasks, and by the late 1930s he had caught the eye of Reinhard Heydrich and Heinrich Himmler and had been promoted from the position of a minor SS functionary to become the chief operational officer and supervisor of the transportation network that carried Jews from Germany and central Europe to concentration and extermination camps in Poland, while also establishing cooperative relations with Nazi-appointed local Jewish leadership councils and cataloging and sending to Berlin huge caches of money and property left behind by victims going to their deaths. Captured by Americans in 1945, he slipped out of a prisoner-of-war camp and, using a series of false names, followed a fantastic escape route beginning in north Germany and ending in an unelectrified house on a dirt road outside of Buenos Aires. There he lived for a decade as Ricardo Klement, hydraulic engineer, rabbit farmer, laundryman, mechanic, husband, and father. His wife and sons, who joined him from Germany in 1952, kept the Eichmann name, which—in conjunction with his fondness for recounting past exploits in company with other escaped Nazis—allowed Israeli secret agents to find him and thus abduct him and fly him to Jerusalem, where, after eleven months of interrogation, he sat in his glass cage. An old boast to his subordinates, recounted at Nuremberg and repeated by him to Nazi cronies in Argentina, that "I will jump into my grave laughing, because the fact that I have the death of five million Jews on my conscience gives me extraordinary satisfaction," was published in *Life* magazine and broadcast around the world before the trial began.[17] Eichmann was a "moral monster," Gideon Hausner, the Polish-born Israeli prosecutor, told reporters. Seeing him in court, however, Martha Gellhorn, anticipating Arendt and many other commentators, asked how it was possible that "a little man with a thin neck, high shoulders, [and] curiously reptilian eyes" had committed such "unrepentant, unlimited, planned evil"?[18] It was a question that Arendt was particularly well equipped to answer.

She was fifty-four years old that spring, a short, chain-smoking intellectual celebrity with an impeccable pedigree and an enormous capacity for work. Born and raised in Germany, she was the child of middle-class, assimilated German Jewish parents. She had been exquisitely well educated in German literature, classical Greek, and ancient and modern philosophy by the great thinkers of the Weimar age, including her friend Karl Jaspers and the charismatic Martin Heidegger. She had recognized and escaped the Nazi peril early, fleeing first to Paris in 1933 and later to New York City, where she lived with her husband, a German gentile called Heinrich Blücher, and spent her leisure hours joyfully cogitating with a "tribe" of distinguished intellectual friends that included Hans Morgenthau, Hans Jonas, Paul Tillich, Lionel and Diana Trilling, Alfred Kazin, Robert Lowell, and Mary McCarthy. She had collected prizes for her books and essays ranging from a Guggenheim Fellowship in 1952 to the prestigious Lessing Prize of the Free City of Hamburg, Germany, in 1959. But she was best known and most deeply respected for her great and difficult work of political history, *The Origins of Totalitarianism,* published in 1951, in which she had traced the rise of the twentieth century's two totalitarian monoliths, Nazism and Stalinism, and analyzed the motives of the men who created them and the men who willingly operated their machinery of murder, especially in Germany. She called these men and their objectives "radically evil," adopting a phrase used by Immanuel Kant, insofar as they attempted to render human individuality — even human law and human existence —"superfluous," without meaning either for the regimes' foot soldiers or their victims.

Arendt had approached the *The New Yorker* for an assignment to write about the Eichmann trial in part to test her theories. She wanted to witness the shape of justice as it would be meted out to one of the Nazi thugs — the deplorable "mass men" and "isolated individuals in an atomized society" who longed to become players in a larger cause, as she described such men in *Origins*[19] — about whom she had thought so long and so deeply, albeit from a distance. "Don't forget how early I left Germany and how little of [the Nazi regime] I really experienced directly," she wrote to Jaspers, explaining her desire to cover the trial for the *The New Yorker.*[20] The elderly philosopher, living in Switzerland, responded with a list of reservations, warning, "The Eichmann trial will be no pleasure for you. I'm afraid it cannot go well."[21] He fretted that the accused might decide not to defend himself but merely say, "Here I stand. It can happen that an eagle falls into the hands of clever trappers," in which case world anti-Semitism, still active if driven below ground, would gain a martyr. Jaspers feared lest a young and vulnerable Israel suffer political harm as a result of the kidnapping and trial, and he cautioned that simple human wisdom might fail when confronted by the historical, political, and legal wrangling that was bound to complicate the trial. "What you will hear will, I fear, depress you and outrage you," he warned.[22] She shared his doubts about potential pitfalls in the conduct of the trial but wrote, "I would never be able to forgive myself if I didn't go and look at this walking disaster [Eichmann] face to face."[23]

She was as celebrated in Jerusalem as she was in America and Europe. She spent evenings with her old friend the former president of the Zionist Federation of Germany Kurt Blumenfeld, her cousin Edna Brocke's family, or Israeli dignitaries. She and Blumenfeld shared a private dinner with the trial's chief judge, Moshe Landau, who—"Marvelous man!" and "the best of German Jewry!"—didn't ordinarily meet with reporters,[24] and she argued deep into the night with Golda Meir, then the Israeli foreign minister, about the need for an Israeli national constitution, like the U.S. Constitution she deeply admired, that would guarantee separation of church and state and equal rights to all.[25]

Arendt had strong confidence in her ability to identify moral principles in the midst of outrage, and she had no particular quarrel with the kidnapping of Eichmann or even with Israel's broadly disputed right to try a German fugitive, whom she considered *hostis humani generis,* an enemy of the human race.[26] One thing she did object to, strongly, was Prime Minister David Ben-Gurion's boasts to the world press that the trial would be conducted as a "show trial" with a triple purpose: to establish a permanent record of the horrors of the Jewish Holocaust, as distinct from other war crimes; to influence world opinion in favor of Israel and against its hostile Arab neighbors, whom he characterized as "disciples of the Nazis";[27] and to instruct young Israelis — born too late to remember Hitler but in time to have watched Israeli soldiers win two regional wars — as to why their parents did not more forcefully resist the Nazi scourge. Additionally, even if the trial were conducted well, she wrote to Jaspers, "I'm afraid that Eichmann will be able to prove, first of all, that no country wanted the Jews (just the kind of Zionist propaganda that Ben-Gurion wants and I consider a disaster) and will demonstrate, second, to what a huge degree the Jews helped organize their own destruction."[28] As it turned out, it was not Eichmann but Arendt who emphasized the last point. She had an old grudge against Ben-Gurion and an even older antipathy to seeing Jews portrayed as defenseless pawns and victims.

About some things, she and Jaspers need not have worried. Eichmann mounted a defense, a surprisingly wily one. But the prosecution's case came first, and it went on for longer and at a higher rhetorical pitch than Arendt could bear to sit through.

The prosecutor Gideon Hausner's argument was straightforward, if rhetorical and contrived ("for publicity purposes") to show Eichmann in the most macabre possible posture. Hausner maintained that the defendant was one in a long line of cruel and fanatical anti-Semites who wished to "destroy, to slay, and to cause [the Jewish people] to perish," beginning with the pharaohs of Egypt and not ending until Israel was created as a nation-state with the legal right to arm and defend an otherwise unprotected people — a point that infuriated Arendt, who saw it as a stratagem to threaten the Jews of the diaspora, including Americans like herself, with a lack of security unless they supported the policies of Israel. Although Eichmann could not be charged with committing mass murder with his own red-spotted hands, as head of the Jewish Affairs Department of the Reich Security Main Office of the SS and thus Hitler's "executive arm for the extermination of the Jewish people," he had dealt a more grievous blow to the Jews than had even such grim figures of barbarism and bloodlust as Genghis Khan, Attila the Hun, and Ivan the Terrible, said Hausner. He may have been seated in a desk chair while conducting mayhem, but he was a mass killer nonetheless. "[I]t was his word that put gas chambers into action; he lifted the telephone, and railroad cars left for the extermination centers," Hausner proclaimed. He was a new kind of predator, "the kind that exercises his bloody craft behind a desk." He was a twentieth-century "desk murderer," brutal and satanic, according to Hausner, who coined the term that was afterward wrongly attributed to Arendt. In the final analysis, Hausner declared, the indicted Nazi lieutenant colonel had been "responsible for everything that happened to the Jewish people [during the Holocaust], from the shores of the Atlantic to the Aegean."[29] The hyperbolic Hausner, Arendt later wrote dismissively, "does his best, his very best, to obey his master,"[30] Prime Minister Ben-Gurion, by summoning an anti-Jewish monster.

Hausner's evidence was extensive and detailed but often beside the point. Hard proof of Eichmann's independent decision-making powers and murderous intent was scarce. The accused had admitted to Israeli interrogators that he was responsible for Jewish deportations in half a dozen European countries; likewise, he admitted to having visited the Nazi killing centers in the east, including Auschwitz, with the clear implication that by 1942, at the latest, he knew the fate of those he ordered into trains. But he had vociferously denied any role in policy making or in the administration of the camps. Hausner felt he had to prove that Eichmann was lying. To this end, he introduced thousands of documents and sworn statements collected during the Nuremberg trials, hoping to build a case for Eichmann's ideological anti-Semitism and for episodes of personal anti-Jewish violence and vengeance during his career. He was only partly successful. The documents were incremental and subject to interpretation and the Nuremberg statements of questionable legitimacy since, Eichmann having been absent from the trials, his captured comrades naturally fell under suspicion of vindicating themselves by blaming him.

Beginning on May 1, Hausner opened a new line of argument to which Arendt objected on principle, calling to the stand nearly one hundred survivors of the Nazi concentration and extermination camps, many of whom were aging or feeble.[31] The harrowing stories they told of forced marches, starvation, gassing, and mass death were the first of their kind ever to be heard in public and served to render unforgettable to civilized listeners around the world the depth of moral and physical degradation inflicted by the Nazis on their hostages and prey. But most of the witnesses had never set eyes on Eichmann or even heard his name during the war years, and none possessed direct evidence against him. Their testimony took place over sixty-two consecutive court sessions with "no apparent bearing on the case," Arendt observed in *Eichmann in Jerusalem,*[32] although their stories did serve all three of Ben-Gurion's objectives. They created a record of Nazi crimes against the Jews of Europe, illustrated the futility of resistance, and demonstrated that the strong arm of Israel was all that protected Jews worldwide from "wind[ing] up in situations where they'll let themselves be slaughtered like sheep," as Arendt complained in a letter to Jaspers.[33] As though to drive home the latter point, Hausner asked many of the elderly, sometimes weeping witnesses why they hadn't fought back. This angered Arendt. "[T]he question the prosecutor regularly addressed to each witness except the [few, mostly youthful] resistance fighters, which sounded so very natural to those who knew nothing of the factual background of the trial, the question 'Why did you not rebel?,'" she wrote in *Eichmann,* "actually served as a smoke screen for the question that was not asked"[34]—the question that would later cause Arendt, who *did* ask, a world of trouble:

Why had the recognized Jewish leadership in so many occupied communities *cooperated* with the Nazis?

"The trial is a real show trial," Arendt remarked in a letter to her husband after the first week of the camp survivors' testimony. She was not unmoved by the witnesses, she wrote, but found the overall effect to be as though the prosecutor were charging not Eichmann "but the whole world" with persecution of the Jews and criminal neglect. "Eichmann is almost forgotten," she noted.[35] Months later, at the sentencing hearing, the judges agreed with her: The testimony of survivors was historically and morally valuable but not relevant in judging Eichmann.

Most of the foreign press and spectators drifted away during this interval; many had work elsewhere. On May 6, Arendt left Jerusalem for Germany and Switzerland, where she gave lectures at German universities, saw old friends, and spent a week with Karl Jaspers and his wife. She and others were back in the reporters' section of the courtroom on June 20, when Eichmann was sworn in and his defense began. She left again for good a mere four days later, traveling first to Zurich to meet her husband and then to Italy for a long-delayed vacation, and missed almost four weeks of Eichmann's testimony and cross-examination by Hausner and the judges.

Eichmann remained in his booth, visibly nervous, as his German lawyer, a former Nuremberg defense attorney named Robert Servatius, gave an opening statement that recapitulated the famous Nuremberg defense. Perhaps predictably, he argued that Eichmann had "neither ordered nor executed" any killings or committed any other crimes under extant law. Moreover, since Eichmann had played no role in *making* the laws under Hitler and yet was legally obliged to follow them, he, too, must be considered by the court to be a victim. Never mind that the argument for forgiveness of universally prohibited actions on the basis of superior orders had been thoroughly rejected at

Nuremberg; it and the claim that Eichmann had not personally killed anyone were the defense's only hope for avoiding a
death sentence. Servatius then questioned Eichmann, drawing
from him over two weeks a tangled, sometimes coy, and alter-
nately self-congratulatory and mock apologetic account of his
SS career throughout the multiple stages of the Nazi destruction of the Jews. His testimony was riddled with apparently
random admissions, stock phrases, mistaken dates, blame of
his superiors, buffoonish professions of goodwill toward Jews,
and bureaucratic mumbo jumbo, which seemed to Arendt to
cause him to grow "paler and more ghostlike" as he spoke.[36] She
thought he possessed a poor memory and a linguistic handicap,
which "amounted to a mild case of aphasia," she wrote. When
he told the court, sorrowfully, "Officialese [amtssprache] is my
only language," she believed him, observing that "officialese became his language because he was genuinely incapable of ut-
tering a single sentence that was not a cliché."[37] If she gave too
much weight to his manner of speaking, it was not merely because she tended to place herself among "the staunchest guard-
ians and partisans of high German culture," as her friend William Barrett remarked,[38] but also because she was accustomed
to finding meaning in the texts she read and heard.

In some ways, Eichmann's defense was more artful than
she or anyone knew. Thousands of pages of transcribed
interviews—full of boasts about his indefatigable devotion to
the Nazi cause—and bitter, anti-Semitic autobiographical writings from the postwar years in Argentina and from his months
of captivity in Israel[39] were ruled inadmissible by the judges or
had yet to be discovered by researchers and scholars. Thus, even
during Gideon Hausner's contentious cross-examination, Eichmann was able to shrewdly embroider his self-portrait as a mid-
level functionary, with no independent authority and with an
earnest wish to befriend the Jews whenever his official duties allowed. As head of the Office of Jewish Affairs in the 1930s, be-

fore Hitler's order to commence the Final Solution, Eichmann testified that he had always done his best to put "soil under the feet of the Jews,"[40] even when expelling them from their ancestral homes — first sending them abroad and then, when Western countries would no longer take them, concocting implausible schemes to resettle them in British-controlled Palestine or on the island of Madagascar before circumstances forced him to transport them to Nisko, Auschwitz, and Theresienstadt. In fact, a major theme of his defense was that he had early on become a specialist in Jewish culture as well as a committed Zionist and an "idealist" who greeted fellow Zionists among the Jews "as equals." When asked by Hausner about the *Life* magazine quote, to the effect that he would die happy because of his role in the slaying of five million Jews, he claimed he had been misquoted and had really said "five million enemies of the Reich," meaning Russians, which made no sense since he had never fought with the German army in the east or had anything to do with the Russians — although he did repeatedly assert, without proof, that he had requested a transfer to combat duty as a soldier after the adoption of the Final Solution. Much later, a full transcript of the "Sassen interviews," conducted in the late 1950s in Argentina and from which the *Life* passage was taken, proved that he was not only lying about the Russians but also considered the *Jews* to be the chief "enemies of the Reich."[41] Arendt, working from the interrogation transcripts and the defendant's recorded testimony, obviously did not believe for a moment that Eichmann was a friend of the Jews. But neither did she view him as a fanatical or ideologically committed racial anti-Semite.[42]

Summing up, Eichmann insisted to the court that he was "humanly but not legally" guilty. He was "humanly guilty" because his strictly technical role in transporting Jews to the death camps resulted in human beings having been killed. But that wasn't his fault. He was legally innocent because, he said, "I had no choice but to carry out the orders I received." His capture and imprisonment — and the near certainty that he would be found guilty — embittered him. He, "exclusively a *receiver* of orders," he whined, was on trial for his life, while those who had issued the orders were happily dead or had otherwise gotten away. "I was merely a little cog in the machinery," Eichmann became famous for saying[43] — a statement that has ever since seemed to cast doubt on the ability of ordinary human beings to remain morally alive in an authoritarian context. Nevertheless, he expressed both surprise and disillusionment when, a few months later, the judges did, in fact, find him guilty of all fifteen counts of the indictment, with a few unproved exceptions, such as inciting violence during Kristallnacht and beating a Jewish child to death in Hungary.[44] According to original research by German scholar Bettina Stangneth, he had reason to be surprised, for he thought that he could get the better of the Jews in Jerusalem. Even before his arrest, as Stangneth demonstrated in her book *Eichmann before Jerusalem: The Unexamined Life of a Mass Murderer* (2014), Eichmann had calculated that if discovered and tried by the Jews, he would be able to trade his life for a plausible account of his actions. That the vaunted Jewish "instinct" for seeking knowledge, as he put it, and a well-known Jewish commitment to universal principles and "intellectualism" always trumped the "sacred egoism of blood" and the right of revenge — a message he had been preaching since the 1930s.[45] These were contemptible weaknesses, according to the Nazi worldview to which he clung; but he was not too proud to manipulate them to his own advantage. He never had been. This time, he was mistaken in his hopes. He lost an appeal to the Israeli Supreme Court and was executed by hanging on May 31, 1962.

Arendt's "Eichmann in Jerusalem" appeared in the *The New Yorker* nine months later as a five-part series. The trial had been nearly forgotten by then, dislodged from memory by the Cuban missile crisis, the American and Russian space race, and the construction of the Berlin Wall. If the eventual book hadn't been so incendiary, and extraordinary, it might have been read by a few, set aside, and remaindered. Instead, thousands of copies are still sold each year, and it remains the starting point for almost every discussion of Eichmann, Arendt, and the Holocaust.

Arendt was fifty-six and again traveling in Europe when "Eichmann in Jerusalem" was published.

There were three great points of controversy that divided readers of the book, as well as many lesser provocations. For the audience of *The New Yorker* and the general reader, the most shocking element was Arendt's persistent, often sarcastic depiction of Eichmann as a joker or a fool, a stammering, sniffling embodiment of "the banality of evil." "Despite all the efforts of the prosecution," she wrote in her opening pages, "everybody could see that this man was not a 'monster,' but it was difficult indeed not to suspect that he was a clown."[46] She pictured him as goofy, vain, "elated" by repetitive clichés, a "joiner,"[47] comically ambitious, and, most notoriously, "thoughtless"—that is, unable to imagine events from anyone else's point of view. Neither innately cruel nor an ideological villain ("not Iago and not Macbeth" and certainly not Richard III, she noted), he was something more disturbing: a person capable of sustained evil action without attendant passion, conviction, concern for others, or remorse. He had no depth, she thought. "Except for an extraordinary diligence in looking out for his personal advancement, he had no motives at all," she wrote in an oft-quoted postscript to the book. "And this diligence in itself was in no way criminal," she added; "he certainly would never have murdered his superior in order to inherit his post. He merely, to put the matter colloquially, never realized what he was doing."[48] If her rhetoric was regrettable (clearly, Eichmann "realized what he was doing" in a legal sense, although he had, perhaps, no particular feeling of recognition for the men and women he did it to), her point was, at the time — the early 1960s — strikingly new and profoundly jarring. That a formerly law-abiding member of the middle class whom not only Arendt and other spectators but also a panel of court-appointed psychiatrists had characterized as "normal"— that is, not a born sociopath or a pervert — could be enlisted to participate in mass "administrative murder," or genocide, was far more frightening to Arendt and to her non-Jewish readers than all the monsters of the deep. (That she was wrong in her particular example did not make her idea wrong, but that's another story.)

She distilled her reflections on the living Eichmann into theory with the subtitle *A Report on the Banality of Evil.* She came to rue the phrase, which originated with her husband, Heinrich Blücher,[49] paying tribute to his old Berlin friend Bertolt Brecht's dramaturgical injunction that "the great political criminals must be exposed, and exposed especially to laughter."[50] (Afterward, Blücher wanted to "punch a few of these people in the nose" who ridiculed her for the formulation, she told Jaspers.)[51] "What did I mean by it?" she later asked.[52] What she *didn't* mean, she insisted, was that evil itself is commonplace.[53] She didn't mean that the Nazi murder machine or its power-driven masterminds, Hitler, Goebbels, and Göring, were ordinary. Still, she *had* changed her mind about the nature of evil. By the banality of evil, "I meant that evil is not *radical* ... that it has no depth," she told *Look* magazine journalist Samuel Grafton in the fall of 1963. She continued: "Evil is a surface phenomenon."[54] In a lecture a month later, she elaborated with a startling analogy. The "hair-raising superficiality" of evil as displayed by Eichmann suggests that evil is infectious. "It can spread over the whole world like a fungus and lay waste precisely because it is not rooted anywhere," she declared to an auditorium packed with students and professors at the University of Chicago.[55]

But mostly she intended the phrase to mark Eichmann as a specimen of the new "mass man," a universal, postindustrial, semi-Marxian type who was characteristically lonely, rootless, socially adrift, economically expendable, and susceptible to both nihilism and authoritarianism.[56] Although she later denied that she had introduced a theoretical element into *Eichmann in Jerusalem* — the book was merely a journalist's report, she told everyone who asked — her reflections on the defendant *became* a theory. This happened at least in part because in the interval between the trial and the publication of the book the social psychologist Stanley Milgram performed and publicized the first of his famous "obedience to authority" experiments at Yale, also in reaction to the Eichmann trial, which seemed to prove that randomly selected clean-cut American college students — in other words, just about anyone — would willingly inflict excruciating pain on their fellows if told by an authority figure that doing so was for the greater good. Together, *Eichmann in Jerusalem* and Milgram's results sent a disturbing message: There is a little Eichmann in all of us. This was explicitly *not* Arendt's premise, but it stuck. To this day, it remains among the most discouraging of commonly held yet sourceless "scientific" truisms.

It is also true that Arendt could not resist constructing a theory. Even in conversation, "she confronted you with the truth," often while sitting in her living room beneath a photograph of a bust of Plato, recalled her admirer Alfred Kazin in his memoir *New York Jew*; "she confronted you with her friendship; she confronted Heinrich even when she joined him in the most passionate seminar I would ever witness between a man and a woman living together; she confronted the gap, the nothingness, the 'extreme situation' of 'modern man.'" For Arendt, "Philosophy was the highest intellectual calling because it was *inescapable,* not a profession but a way of life."[57]

At least since 1933, not only philosophy but also political theory was a way of life for Arendt, though in a broad, almost Greek sense — politics considered as an art conferring honor in the public sphere.[58] But she sometimes took up less agnostic political positions. The book's second controversy was over her derisive references to the government of Israel, encapsulated in snide remarks about David Ben-Gurion and Gideon Hausner and in an unwelcome comparison of Israel's religious prohibition against Jewish intermarriage with the Nazi laws banning sexual contact and marriage between Jews and Germans; that Israel did not have a written constitution, she acidly observed, could be explained, in part, by a reluctance to spell out such a racially biased law in a national civic document.[59] Criticism of Israel, then as now, was considered dangerous and disloyal.

Arendt had been a dedicated and hardworking Zionist activist in the 1930s and 1940s. In 1948, however, she had spoken out against Israel's founding as a strictly Jewish state, warning of institutional injustice, militarism, and dependency on foreign powers as the probable price of excluding Arabs from citizenship in a negotiated binational state. Her Jewish friends were grumpily familiar with her renegade views on Israel. What surprised and galled them and Jewish advocacy groups was *Eichmann in Jerusalem*'s handling of a more deeply buried and far more sensitive issue: the role of Jews themselves in the implementation of the Final Solution. That she discussed this issue openly and pejoratively — and in the pages of *The New Yorker*, amid the ads for Peck & Peck, Dry Sack, and resorts in the Bahamas — many could not forgive, even to this day.

If Hausner's question to camp survivors "Why did you not rebel?" was provocative, it was also rhetorical; the answer was obvious. How much more provocative and vexing was Arendt's harsh rejoinder to it, embedded in a forty-page discussion of the fascinating question of whether Adolf Eichmann had a conscience. Arendt concluded that Eichmann did have a conscience, a relatively normal one that operated during most of his life but that went on functioning for only a few weeks after the Final Solution became official Nazi policy in 1942.[60] And why did his conscience stop working after a few weeks? The

Nazi "specialist in Jewish affairs" claimed that no one, "no one at all,"[61] had protested the policy or refused to cooperate with it, including local Jewish leaders, whom he had carefully organized into Nazi-approved leadership councils called Judenräte. Arendt seemed to agree. That ordinary Jews could *not* rebel she did not doubt; they had no training, no weapons, and very little information about their destinations or their fate. But that was not "the whole truth," she asserted in the most infamous and acrimonious passage of *Eichmann in Jerusalem*. By mid-1942, the Jewish leadership of Europe did know where Eichmann's trains were going. And yet:

> In Amsterdam as in Warsaw, in Berlin as in Budapest, Jewish officials could be trusted to compile the lists of persons and of their property, to secure money from the deportees to defray the expenses of their deportation and extermination, to keep track of vacated apartments, to supply police forces to help seize Jews and get them on trains, until, as a last gesture, they handed over the assets of the Jewish community in good order for final confiscation.

In the magazine and in the original edition of the book — but not in later editions — she added, quoting damning material from a secondary source:

> They distributed the Yellow Star badges, and sometimes, as in Warsaw, "the sale of the armbands became a regular business; there were ordinary armbands of cloth and fancy plastic armbands which were washable." In the Nazi-inspired, but not Nazi-dictated, manifestoes they issued, we still can sense how they enjoyed their new power — "The Central Jewish Council has been granted the right of absolute disposal over all Jewish spiritual and material wealth and over all Jewish manpower" — as the first announcement of the Budapest Council phrased it.[62]

One can almost sense how Arendt enjoyed her fury while writing this remarkably uncharitable passage. She concluded:

> Wherever Jews lived there were recognized Jewish leaders, and this leadership, almost without exception, cooperated in one way or another, for one reason or another, with the Nazis. The whole truth was that if the Jewish people had really been unorganized and leaderless, there would have been chaos and plenty of misery but the total number of victims would hardly have been between four and a half and six million people.[63]

"To a Jew," she wrote in another famous passage, "this role of the Jewish leaders in the destruction of their own people is undoubtedly the darkest chapter of the whole dark story."[64] Hardly, remarked her critics, who were many.

It was an odd thing for Arendt to do—one of the oddest things she had done in a lifetime of conscious rebellion. For she herself had warned against it. Early in the book, criticizing Gideon Hausner's histrionics and his indiscriminate witness list, she insisted that the trial must be conducted in the American manner, with an absolute focus on the innocence or guilt of the accused. "Justice demands that [Eichmann] be prosecuted, defended, and judged," she wrote, "and that all the other questions of seemingly greater import . . . of 'Why the Jews?' and 'Why the Germans?,' . . . of 'How could the Jews through their own leaders cooperate in their own destruction?' . . . be left in abeyance."[65] That she didn't leave the issue of the Jewish councils in abeyance—although the Israeli prosecutor largely did—can be explained by only an unwillingness, in the midst of thinking and writing, to admit that all the Jews of Europe had been powerless and helpless, a condition that in the span of her life, with its many hardships and uncertainties, Arendt had not once discovered in herself.

To many of her friends, admirers, and allies, Arendt, the quixotic, dark-eyed, Greek-reading, Goethe-quoting, deep-thinking German Jewish public intellectual — an awe-inspiring presence in New York and European Jewish literary circles — had simply delivered a brutal insult to the Jewish people. She had openly blamed the educated Jews of Europe for aiding in the overwhelming devastation while seeming to let the awful avatar of evil, Adolf Eichmann, off the hook.

This was not literally so. Arendt, like the panel of judges in Jerusalem, affirmed that Eichmann was guilty of genocide and must be put to death. But her reasoning was so consciously based on universal principles and so little on anger that, paradoxically, it almost missed its mark. Speaking in the voice of judgment itself in the epilogue of *Eichmann in Jerusalem,* and dismissing the question of whether Eichmann knew what he was doing ("for politics is not like the nursery; in politics obedience and support are the same," she wrote),[66] she addressed Eichmann directly: "And just as you supported and carried out a policy of not wanting to share the earth with the Jewish people and the people of a number of other nations — as though you and your superiors had any right to determine who should and who should not inhabit the world — we find that no one, that is, no member of the human race, can be expected to want to share the earth with you. That is the reason, and the only reason, you must hang." These were the final, somewhat mystifying words of *Eichmann in Jerusalem,* written months after Eichmann had been executed in Ramie Prison in Israel and his ashes scattered in the Mediterranean Sea. She hanged him for a second time, which might have mollified her critics but did not. Until the book's two final sentences, the paragraphs pronouncing her judgment of Eichmann hummed with the pulse of Immanuel Kant's categorical imperative, also known as the Golden Rule, which insists that each of us, to the degree that we are moral, may take only those actions we would willingly see become a universal law — liars living in a world without honesty or trust, Nazi trainmasters also loaded into trains. Adhering to a state-sanctioned law offers no exemption, in Arendt's view, because a law can be unjust and therefore wrong to act upon. When every person is a legislator, thinking is mandatory. Eichmann's first crime, therefore, was *not thinking*; and Arendt would spend the remaining twelve years of her life working to explain just what kinds of thinking, judging, and acting conscious people must partake in to be members in good standing of a diverse and moral human race.

Almost two years passed between the end of the Eichmann trial and the publication of *Eichmann in Jerusalem*. They were eventful years for Arendt. In the fall of 1961, Heinrich Blücher — "my four walls," as she called her husband — a rough-and-tumble sixty-two-year-old autodidact and self-created sage of New York's Bard College, fell ill with a ruptured brain aneurism, one of a series of debilitating events that left him vulnerable to weakness and depression. While the Eichmann verdict was being read by the judges in Jerusalem in December 1961, Arendt was commuting between her own teaching duties at Wesleyan University in Connecticut and their shared apartment on Riverside Drive in New York, where Blücher gradually recovered strength. In March 1962, she herself was laid low. She was crossing Central Park in the backseat of a taxicab, reading,[67] when a truck rammed into the cab, knocked her unconscious, and left her with a concussion, nine fractured ribs, a hemorrhaged eye, broken teeth, and damaged heart muscles. She was restricted to bed rest and mild activity for the next two months, but her heart never entirely healed. Nonetheless, between the summer of 1961 and January 1963 she published two ambitious and well-regarded books, *Between Past and Future: Six Exercises in Political Thought* and *On Revolution,* a comparative study of the American and French Revolutions, before finally publishing the

275-page *Eichmann in Jerusalem* in the late winter and spring of 1963.

It was partly as a result of an insurance settlement from the taxi accident that she was in Europe when the five-part series appeared in *The New Yorker* in February and March 1963, alongside Peter Arno's waspish cartoons, book and theater reviews, and short stories by John Cheever and William Maxwell. Beginning with the third installment, which featured her reflections on the Jewish councils, it was as if a bomb had gone off within those stately pages. Arendt was in Basel, helping to celebrate Karl Jaspers's eightieth birthday, when William Shawn, the editor of *The New Yorker,* sent a telegram that read like one of the magazine's understated cartoon captions: "People in town seem to be discussing little else."[68] Soon thereafter, a lawyer and former Israeli government finance official, representing the Council of Jews from Germany in Israel, showed up in Basel demanding that she tell Viking Press to halt the publication of the book, scheduled for May, which she decidedly refused to do. The council issued a "declaration of war" against her. These were early warning signs. In May, she met Blücher for a tour of Greece and Italy, ending in Paris. While they were traveling, her friends Mary McCarthy and Hans Morgenthau and her German-speaking personal assistant Lotte Kohler kept her apprised of the gathering storm in New York, but it was only when she and Blücher returned to the city in early summer that the full force of the organized anger and what Jaspers later called attempts at "ambush" became clear to her.

She was at first bemused by the tall stacks of unopened mail that greeted her in their West Side apartment, some of it "interesting," she told Jaspers, much of it spiteful and even foul.[69] One letter, accusing her of desecrating "the souls of our six million martyrs," warned that the ghosts of the dead would swarm about her day and night, giving her no rest.[70] The reviews, which she hadn't seen, were overwhelmingly negative.

One early diatribe in the *Jewish Spectator* bore the headline "Self-Hating Jewess Writes Pro-Eichmann Series for *The New Yorker*," and another, in the *Jewish Floridian*, indicted her for "digging future Jewish graves to the applause of the world's unconverted anti-Semites."[71] The *New York Times*, abandoning tradition, assigned the book to an interested party: Judge Michael Musmanno, an outspoken former American jurist at Nuremberg whose testimony for the prosecution at the Eichmann trial—in which he recalled an absurd jailhouse allegation by the Nazi Joachim von Ribbentrop that Hitler's decision to murder millions of Jews was attributable to the influence of Eichmann—Arendt had disparaged in the book. Unsurprisingly, Musmanno bitterly depreciated her, contorting her thesis to include "that Eichmann was not really a Nazi at heart, that the Gestapo were helpful to the Jews, and that, all in all, Eichmann was really a modest man" who ought not to have been punished at all—a summary that would become rote among the book's enemies.[72]

More distressing were the scathing reviews by erstwhile friends and colleagues in periodicals that had proudly published her work for many years. Her earliest published reports and columns in the United States had appeared in a German-language newspaper called *Aufbau*; now, in a series of ill-natured articles, *Aufbau* excoriated *Eichmann* and Arendt and refused to publish any response from her. In *Partisan Review,* to which she had contributed some of her best essays in English, the playwright and critic Lionel Abel mocked her reporting, cast doubt on her truthfulness, and declared *The Origins of Totalitarianism* also "invalidated" by the shoddy quality of her thinking in *Eichmann.* Arendt never wrote for *Partisan Review* again—not, she explained to McCarthy, because of the review itself but because she believed that the editors, once friends, had known that Abel disliked and would attack her; "Hannah Arrogant," he called her behind her back. *Newsweek, Commentary,* the *Times Lit-*

erary Supplement, Dissent, and other leading magazines chastised her for "flagrant and major errors," "gross inaccuracies,"[73] and making unattributed use of original research from Raul Hilberg's immense but heretofore unheralded 1961 work of history, *The Destruction of the European Jews,* without proper attribution; in subsequent editions, Arendt added citations to the book. Former admirers admonished her for hard-heartedness and moral deafness. "To kill millions is banal; any one of us could do it under the pressures of a totalitarian state," wrote the sharp-tongued polemicist Marie Syrkin in *Dissent.* "But to be among the sufferers is somehow culpable; any one of us would have faced death more valiantly, else what point is there to the author's accusations?"[74]

Mary McCarthy inadvertently raised the ante by mounting a defense of her friend in her snappiest, if not her soundest, style, both at editorial gatherings and in print. "When I read *Eichmann in Jerusalem* in *The New Yorker* last winter I thought it splendid and extraordinary," she warbled in an essay in *Partisan Review.* "I still do. But apparently this is because I am a Gentile." Non-Jews liked the book, she had noticed, while Jews hated it. "It is as if *Eichmann in Jerusalem* had required a special pair of Jewish spectacles to make its 'true purport' visible," she wrote.[75] Marie Syrkin replied that this might be the case simply because Jews predominated among those who actually knew something about the subject. Syrkin went on:

> But Miss McCarthy does not let it go at that. She tells us that she found Miss Arendt's account of the extermination of six million Jews "morally exhilarating" and that she heard in it "heavenly music, like that of the final chorus of *Figaro* or the *Messiah,*" because of the "happy endings," the episodes in which a few Jews were saved. Miss McCarthy's acoustics are, to say the least, remarkable. She would probably suggest that a special Gentile hearing aid is required for the reception of these higher registers. Jews

are too deafened by the cries of a million shot and gassed children
to appreciate the full angelic orchestration enjoyed by Miss Mc-
Carthy.[76]

Debates were vicious and ongoing, staged in New York hotels,
lecture halls, and living rooms; one, which included a pacific
Raul Hilberg, broke up into shouting matches. For months, as
Irving Howe recalled, a "civil war" raged among the city's and
the nation's intellectuals.[77]

The war had numerous fronts. Friendships — chief among
them Arendt's friendship with Hans Jonas, a fellow émigré, an
ally, and an adorer from her youth — were ruptured. In addi-
tion, "three or four large organizations, along with whole regi-
ments of 'scholarly' assistants and secretaries, are busying themselves ferreting out mistakes I made," she wrote to Jaspers. The
organizations included the American Jewish Committee, the
World Jewish Congress, and B'nai B'rith, as well as the State of
Israel itself, which sent Gideon Hausner to New York to speak
out against her "throwing stones at the victims."[78] One such
belligerent "assistant," Jacob Robinson, a former "special con-
sultant on Jewish affairs" at Nuremberg and an adviser to the
prosecution at the Eichmann trial, published a four-hundred-
page directory of what he claimed were factual mistakes, mis-
construed statistics, and quotes out of context in *Eichmann in
Jerusalem*.[79] The book, called *And the Crooked Shall Be Made
Straight: The Eichmann Trial, the Jewish Catastrophe, and Hannah Arendt's Narrative,* was worshipfully reviewed by Robinson's acquaintance Walter Laqueur in the recently founded *New
York Review of Books*. Until then, Arendt had remained silent in
print. Now she counterpunched, also in the *New York Review
of Books,* keenly ridiculing Robinson's supposed "eminence"
as a historian and listing *his* many errors, both of fact and of
interpretation.

Arendt proved a fierce intellectual battler on her own behalf.

She condemned the united campaign of Jewish establishment forces and the Israeli government ("together with its consulates, embassies, missions, etc., throughout the world") against her. She impugned their motives, for good reason, and doubted their judgment: "Thus, with the unerring precision with which a bicyclist on his first ride will collide with the obstacle he is most afraid of, Mr. Robinson's formidable supporters have put their whole power at the service of propagating what they were most anxious to avoid"—publicity about the role of the previous generation of Jewish leaders in the massacre of the Jews. In the end, she wrote, "the men who stand guard over facts are not the officers of interest groups ... but the reporters, the historians, and finally the poets."[80] In a cool and combative essay, her appeal to the truthfulness of poetry was her only show of heart.

The Eichmann scandal grew "to fantastic proportions."[81] Rabbis preached against her from the pulpit.[82] Prime Minister Ben-Gurion circulated a reproving letter to American Jews who had defended her and was rumored to have expressed his displeasure against her to the Kennedy administration. Her public bravado masked a deepening private shock and horror at being singled out and cast into a garish public light. She became concerned that she or Blücher or both—but particularly Blücher, a former German Communist with a dangerous past—might lose their American citizenship, gained in 1951 and 1952, respectively, after a decade of striving. That fall, Blücher's health, never good, began to fail again, with emergent signs of heart disease; the premature old age of her beloved husband and "four walls" became "an extremely palpable reality," she confided to a friend.[83] From universal veneration by her peers and a sure sense of safety, she had oddly fallen. She wasn't exactly sure why, although she had a hypothesis about "dirty laundry to hide" at the highest levels of the Jewish power structure.[84] She had not felt herself so uncertain in her orientation in the world or so close to open ostracism, to what she liked to call "pariah-dom," or to personal vulnerability since arriving penniless in the United States in 1941 — or perhaps since her sometimes sorrowful childhood.

It didn't help her reputation among Jews when, in the 1980s and 1990s, letters she had written during the trial itself were published. In a letter to Jaspers, she had ranked the judges and lawyers by nationality. The supreme court justices were "the best of German Jewry." Hausner, a "typical Galician Jew," was "probably one of those people who don't know any language." She despised "the oriental mob" that hung around in front of the courthouse and "a police force that gives me the creeps, speaks only Hebrew, and looks Arabic."[85] Her German snobbery was on display, a not uncommon outcome of her Prussian Jewish upbringing — or so her cousin Edna Brocke explained it. "Some of her best friends were Ostjuden [Eastern Jews in Poland]. But the moment it became a matter of political might [in Israel], all these things came up from her guts."[86]

Arendt's reluctance to identify with Eastern European Jews and other scapegoats was not necessarily hypocrisy or a fault of character. It may have been her excessive belief in the virtues of pariahhood — that is, she may have gone too far in her own defiance of others' expectations and conventions. If she could not admit that the Jews were wholly innocent, it may have been because that would have made *her* a victim, too. In any case, it got her into trouble.

As the Eichmann controversy slowly receded over the next few years, two things continued to haunt her. One was a bitter exchange of letters with the eminent historian of Jewish mysticism Gershom Scholem. Arendt had known Scholem, who was a Berliner by birth and upbringing, since the 1930s; he had been a boyhood friend of her deceased friend Walter Benjamin, whose companionship and literary enthusiasms she had cherished. On reading *Eichmann,* Scholem told Arendt that she had put so much emphasis on Jewish weakness that "your account ceases to be objective and acquires overtones of malice." Since he regarded her "wholly as a daughter of our people, and in no other way," he lamented "the heartless, frequently almost sneering and malicious tone with which these matters, touching the very quick of our life, are treated in your book," adding, "In the Jewish tradition there is a concept, hard to define and yet concrete enough, which we know as *Ahabath Israel*: 'Love of the Jewish people. . . .' In you, dear Hannah, as in so many intellectuals who came from the German Left, I find little trace of this."[87] He signed the letter Gershom, his Hebrew name.

She answered, addressing him as Gerhard, his German name. She had never been a member of the German Left, she pointed out (although her husband had been). She took umbrage at his seeing her "wholly" as a daughter of the Jewish people. Was he implying that she denied that she was Jewish? That would be as pointless as denying she was a woman. And yet the "Jewish problem" had never been her problem, she claimed, for "I have always regarded my Jewishness as [simply] one of the indisputable factual data of my life" and nothing more, a declaration that might strike those who knew the facts of her life as radiating both intellectual truth and emotional amnesia and bravado. As for *Ahabath Israel,* she told him, he was quite right. She did not love *any* people or collective—"neither the German people, nor the French, nor the American, nor the working class"—but only persons, specifically her friends. "[I]t is incomprehensible to me why you should wish to stick a label on me which never fitted in the past and does not fit now."[88] That she was sui generis—a *conscious* and brilliant outsider for whom conventional reactions and ordinary rules of decorum had little meaning—shouted from the pages of her letter to her former friend.

One remark offered a particularly rich insight into the passion that Scholem mistook for malice in her condemnation of the Jewish councils. "[W]rong done by my own people naturally grieves me more than wrong done by other peoples," she wrote. "This grief, however, in my opinion is not for display, even if it should be the innermost motive for certain actions and attitudes." Grieving invites vulnerability; discovering truth is a motive that yields strength. "She was very astonished that so many other people didn't see the truth, *her* truth," in the *Eichmann* book, recalled Brocke. "She never thought what this same truth — what it could do to other people."[89] On the whole, she wanted to be judged in all the three-dimensionality of a fully human being. She disliked the caricature of Jews as supernally gifted and only therefore deserving (all "the customary chauvinistic stuff of the assimilationists, then and now")[90] almost as much as she disliked the stereotype of Jews as helpless victims.

Scholem published their letters, not only in Jerusalem, as she had agreed, but also, without permission, in the widely read British arts magazine *Encounter*. They never spoke to each other again. The exchange "finished for me . . . the question about the character of Hannah," Scholem wrote to their mutual friend Daniel Bell in 1980, four years after Arendt's death.[91] His sentiment that it "was one of the most bitter controversies of my life" was true for Arendt as well.

There were other casualties. In May 1963, when the scandal was still new, Arendt traveled from a hotel in Sicily[92] to Jerusalem to try to patch things up with her oldest and perhaps most deeply cherished friend, Kurt Blumenfeld. She had not seen him since the trial. Now he was ill and dying. Although he had not read *Eichmann,* others had told him about it. She had heard that he was angry, even outraged, and that he had had to be talked out of denouncing the book from his deathbed. Edna Brocke drove her to see Blumenfeld in the hospice where he spent his final days; Arendt believed that if she could explain her ideas to him he would not be angry. Whether she spoke with him is not clear. Brocke remembers that she did not, either because he refused to see her or because his wife and children objected.[93] Her friend and first biographer Elisabeth Young-Bruehl stated that she and Blumenfeld did have an exchange of words.[94] In either case, there was no rapprochement. Arendt returned to Brocke's parents' home by taxi, "a sad and broken person," Brocke recalled.

Blumenfeld died four days later.

2

Death of the Father

Königsberg, 1906–1923

Every thought is an afterthought.

— HANNAH ARENDT, in an interview with Gunter Gaus, 1964[1]

I F EICHMANN WAS a joiner, Hannah Arendt was singular and often solitary from childhood.

She was born on October 14, 1906, in Germany, the only child of Paul and Martha Arendt, and she grew up in a pre–World War I atmosphere of high standards, principled ideals, and social and political optimism of a kind that is now difficult to reconstruct. Mozart, Goethe, and ancient German fairy tales were household entertainments. Personal achievement was so sternly taken for granted that "any [stated] ambition was taken to be inferior," Arendt remembered years later.[2] "I was brought up under the assumption: *Das Moralische versteht sich von selbst* — moral conduct is a matter of course."[3] Her childhood was spent in what turned out to be the final years of the most favorable time and place in modern European history to be a gifted child and also to be a Jew.

She came from a proud tradition, and this contributed much to her self-confidence and even arrogance as a public intellectual. She was the granddaughter and great-granddaughter of prosperous Russian Jewish merchants and traders who had

left czarist Russia for Germany during the Jewish Enlightenment and settled in Königsberg, a fairy-tale city built around
a central castle at the far eastern edge of Prussia on the Baltic
Sea, less than one hundred miles from the Russian border. Her
mother's parents, the Cohns, owned a thriving tea-trading firm,
the largest private company in Königsberg. Her paternal grandfather, Max Arendt, was a retired merchant and popular town
civic leader. Her parents belonged to the first large generation
of religiously agnostic, politically liberal, highly educated German Jewish professionals since the Jewish emancipation of 1812
in Prussia; their friends and peers were doctors, lawyers, judges,
psychologists, and scientists. Paul studied engineering at the
city's Albertina University, where Immanuel Kant had once held
court and Moses Mendelssohn lectured.[4] Martha completed her
training in music and French during three years spent abroad
in Paris. When their bright-eyed only child Hannah was born,
they could imagine so few obstacles to her happiness based on
her Jewish ethnicity that, as Hannah later confided to an interviewer, "My parents didn't tell me that I was Jewish," until she
began to venture from home.[5] Although she later declined to
identify herself either by her ethnicity or by her nationality at
birth, like other children of her time and background, including
future friends such as Bruno Bettelheim, Hans Jonas, and Albert Einstein, she grew up thinking of herself as German.

    She was born in the central German town of Linden, near
Hannover, where her father worked as an electrical engineer in
one of the booming pre–World War I industrial hubs of Germany. During the two and a half years she lived in Linden, a
sense of comfort reigned: In a tall house on a lively square, surrounded by her father's library of prized Greek and Latin texts,
by her mother's music, and by the ministrations of a Christian
nursemaid, she was as sheltered as a child could be. Her notably warmhearted and doting mother — an adherent of Goethe's
progressive theories of childrearing and a sympathizer with left-

wing political causes, including the ideas of the socialist Sparta-cist League founder Rosa Luxemburg — sang and read aloud to the dark-haired little girl, whose infant "inner awakening" she tracked in a baby book. As a toddler, Hannah was a fluent bab-bler, and by age six had become a tiny phenomenon of abstract thinking, with a penchant for arithmetic and a preference for musical theory over practice. Yet exile, a pivotal theme in the daughter's adult life and work, also began early: Even before she could speak in full sentences, she was cast out of the predictable security of what her mother called a "sunshine" childhood into dislocation and confusion. Her parents moved from Linden back to their own birthplace of Königsberg, the first of many dislodgments that would supply her with perhaps her great-est theme: the vulnerability of the rootless ones — read: almost everyone — in modern life.

Illness caused the move. Hannah's father had syphilis, con-tracted before his marriage in 1902. He and Martha had dis-cussed the risks of syphilis in marriage and childbearing, but the disease was not well understood until later in the decade, and they assumed that the rapid disappearance of his early symp-toms after standard treatment (consisting of induction of a ma-larial fever) meant permanent remission or a cure. The disease, however, was merely in its latent phase. The telltale signs of pro-gression gradually appeared. By 1909, he was exhibiting weak-ness in his legs and arms and could no longer work, so he, his wife, and Hannah returned to Königsberg, where they had a large extended family[6] and easy proximity to the university hos-pital. Hannah was almost three; her father lived for another four and a half years, until just after her seventh birthday. His symptoms were progressive and grim, beginning with a loss of balance so that he stumbled and fell unexpectedly in public and involving disfiguring rashes, sores, and tumors, as well as mental deterioration characterized by seizures, paralysis, mania, and fi-nally dementia and death. Hannah spent almost every day with her father, first in the house her parents purchased on a tree-lined street in Königsberg and later in a psychiatric hospital, until in the end he failed to recognize her. His untamed moods, his helplessness, his derangement, and his suffering must have frightened the small girl, but according to her mother's diary she did not show fear or repugnance: "She prayed for him mornings and nights without having been taught to do so"— except, perhaps, by the Christian nursemaid. "She takes [her father's death] to be something sad for me," Martha wrote. "She herself remains untouched by it."[7]

Of course, the little girl did not remain untouched by her father's misery and death.[8] It was the crucial separation of her life, preparing her for others. During the next few years she suffered chronic ear and throat infections, coughs, and fevers whenever her mother left home to travel, as she often did, on shopping and cultural trips to Paris and Berlin. "A child should not be separated from its mother," Hannah lectured Martha at age four, when her father's symptoms were intensifying.[9] From then until her teens, every six months she had to be tested for congenital syphilis, using the new Wassermann test, which involved drawing blood or spinal fluid and was notorious for false positives; in a child who relished and was increasingly praised for her mental gifts, this surely engendered fear and its stately sister, fortitude. The source of Paul's deterioration could not have remained a family secret even if his illness had not progressed in public: Friends and associates of Hannah's grandparents, aunts, uncles, and cousins in the small world of respectable Jewish Königsberg would have known that Paul was dying of what was then considered a "pariah's disease" and believed to be spread by prostitutes, as would have many of the friends Hannah made among her peers as she grew up. If Hannah learned how not to show vulnerability — how to hide fear, grief, and shame — it was because she had a painful early "sense of being ostracized," as she wrote to her professor Martin Heidegger a decade later, in an autobiographical essay she called "The Shadows." In the essay, she refers to the slow acquisition of an emotional shell in childhood that provided protection if not comfort. Although "her sensitivity and vulnerability... grew to almost grotesque proportions," she wrote, misfortunes that might strike at a "defenseless person" did not wound her. "Everything that happened to her... made its way deep into her soul and remained there, isolated and sealed off."[10] For her, early suffering gradually yielded some powerful defensive traits: self-reliance, defiance, aggressive pride, and what her university friend Hans Jonas called a "know-it-all attitude" under stress.[11] Much later still, in an essay celebrating the writer Isak Dinesen (whose father had also suffered from syphilis, as Dinesen did, too), she praised the art of storytelling as an antidote to pain. But she never told the story of her father's illness to anyone except, perhaps, her second husband, Heinrich Blücher, to whom she confided almost everything; nor did she write about it. The most she ever said publicly or to friends was that her father had died young.[12]

Paul Arendt died on October 30, 1913. The following August, Germany declared war on Russia and World War I commenced. Finding themselves less than a day's train ride from the enemy's western border, Martha, Hannah, and their extended family joined thousands of other Königsbergers who packed their bags into railway carriages and headed west to central Germany and safety. The mother and daughter spent ten weeks in Berlin, until it became clear that the Russian army would not invade Königsberg, and then returned.

Hannah, eight years old in the fall of 1914, lived at home with Martha for the remainder of the war, but the material abundance of early childhood gave way to severe wartime shortages of food and fuel, heavily restricted trade and travel, chronic cold, illness, and isolation. As the tide of war turned against Germany, the wealth of the Arendts and Cohns, built on trade with Russia, shrank — to such an extent that by 1918 or 1919, Martha's inherited family income could no longer support mother and daughter in their middle-class home. Martha took in a boarder to help pay expenses and then, in 1920, she accepted an offer of marriage from a working-class Jewish widower named Martin Beerwald. Self-made, uneducated, and floridly conventional, Beerwald was the son of a Russian money lender and a partner in an ironmongery business belonging to his brother-in-law; courting Martha, he took her for Sunday drives in the firm's wooden trucking cart, pulled by workhorses. After the wedding, Martha and thirteen-year-old Hannah went to live with Beerwald and his two grown daughters in a house two blocks and a world away from the one in which Hannah had lived with and cared for her father.

Her sense of displacement and resentment was acute. Not surprisingly, she did not adapt. She bridled at sharing her mother's attention with her stepfather and stepsisters. Beerwald wasn't as well educated or affluent as the Arendts and Cohns had been, but he offered Hannah and her mother a degree of financial security amid the tumultuous — and ultimately disastrous — postwar economic chaos of defeated Germany and presumably expected conventional good behavior in return. Hannah threw tantrums and rebelled, at one point sneaking out of the house, against parental orders, to spend the night in a distant town with a new friend of hers named Anne Mendelssohn, a descendant of Moses Mendelssohn and his grandson Felix, to whom Hannah remained attached all her life. Beerwald, with his Bismarckian mustache and traditional sense of paternal authority, reacted with frustration to her willfulness, intellectual precocity, hauteur, and moodiness — her "dreamy, enchanted isolation," as she described her adolescent state of mind in "The Shadows." As a stay against "dull pain," she immersed herself in reading and writing poetry and in the study of German, Greek, and Latin. She gathered a group of school friends and cousins, including Edna Brocke's father, Ernst Fuerst, into a

"Greek Circle," modeled on study groups then popular in German universities, to translate Homeric hexameters in her Beerwaldian bedroom. She "read everything," including the works of Kant and Karl Jaspers, Anne Mendelssohn recalled,[13] and was by this time a slender, dark-eyed magnet for exceptionally gifted boys. Her first boyfriend, Ernst Grumach, Anne Mendelssohn's cousin, was four years her senior, a doctoral student in philology at Albertina University and a future Goethe scholar. From fifteen on, every brilliant boy who met her fell in love. Soon, brilliant men, among them Martin Heidegger, would nudge the boys aside.

If Hannah's parents hadn't told her she was Jewish, she learned it soon enough from Max Arendt, her paternal grandfather, and was reminded of it by the city's Christian population, for no part of Germany or of Europe was entirely free from anti-Semitism, even in relatively peaceful times and far from the centers of power. Max, a former chairman of the Königsberg city council, was Hannah's almost daily companion during her father's darkest days, until he, too, succumbed to illness a few months before Paul's death. In describing her childhood, she sometimes confused the two men, remembering long, happy walks with Paul that had actually taken place with Max. A mainstay of the city's Reform synagogue, Max took her with him to weekly Shabbat services. He was also an active member of the Central Association of German Citizens of Jewish Faith, an organization founded in Berlin in the 1890s to combat anti-Semitism that also strongly opposed Zionism, and he was an avid debater with the young Kurt Blumenfeld, then a law student at Albertina University and a Zionist student organizer. As a child, Hannah would have heard the two men arguing over the burgeoning movement to establish a Jewish homeland in Palestine. Max, like many more or less assimilated Jews, saw no real conflict between his German and Jewish heritage and scoffed at the idea of living outside his native country. "[He] would not hear any argument that cast his Germanness in doubt," wrote Elisabeth Young-Bruehl.[14] "When my Germanness is attacked, I prepare for murder," Blumenfeld remembered Max exclaiming.[15] Blumenfeld, who in the 1930s headed the Zionist Federation of Germany, played on the floor with Hannah in her toddler years, flirted with her in her twenties, recruited her for the Zionist research work that would bring about her flight from Germany in 1933, and loved her as a daughter until *Eichmann* appeared in print. On this basis alone, it's clear that Hannah was conscious not only that she was a Jew but also that being Jewish was problematical, if not particularly troublesome or a mark of being "inferior," something she told the German interviewer Günter Gaus that she had never felt or been made to feel.[16]

There is another layer of this story. Blumenfeld, whose parents, a judge and a musician, resembled Hannah's—liberal, sophisticated, assimilated—was less intent than an earlier generation of Zionists had been on improving the lives of impoverished Russian and Polish Jews, or Ostjuden;[17] his aim was to bring the spirit of Zionism and Jewish solidarity to middle-class men and women like his and Hannah's parents, who he believed had lost their sense of Jewish identity and hence their source of spiritual sustenance and sense of meaning.[18] In a European culture that viewed all Jews with scorn, however muted or camouflaged, and evoked shame if not terror in many Jews, there was little to separate Ostjuden from assimilated Jewry, he believed. Much later, Hannah came at least partly to agree with him. But as a youth she made a reasonable distinction between herself and those who were uneducated and derided. Anti-Semitism "poisoned the souls of many" children, she explained to Gaus in 1964, but it did not poison hers: "My mother was always convinced that you mustn't let it get to you." When local children issued taunts, Martha expected her to handle them.[19] When her teachers made anti-Semitic comments, on the other hand, Hannah recalled that her mother instructed her to leave the classroom and walk home; Martha would then write "one of her many registered letters" to the school authorities. In this way, she said, she retained her dignity. Still, the objectionable comments were "mostly not about me, but about other Jewish girls, eastern Jewish students in particular," she recalled — girls who dressed differently and hadn't mastered the German language.

Before a new wave of Zionism arrived in the 1910s, embodied by Max's friend Blumenfeld, many established Jews felt Ostjuden to be at the heart of what was commonly — and ominously — called the "Jewish Question." In her youth she "found the so-called Jewish question boring." Hannah wrote to Karl Jaspers in adulthood: "By virtue of my background I was simply naïve."[20] Yet even as an adult she could privately show distaste for Eastern Europeans. Another rule of conduct Hannah may have absorbed was — at least when no one was under attack — not to let herself be mistaken for the Jewish girls her teachers mocked. She would not be a victim.

In any case, she learned to stand up for herself with enviable conviction. At age fifteen, angered by something one of her teachers said, she attempted to organize a boycott of the teacher's classes and was instead expelled from school. Martha, who often took her daughter's side, arranged for her to complete her secondary schooling at the University of Berlin. Thus the girl escaped the Beerwald household and began a ten-year course of study with some of Europe's great thinkers, including the Catholic existential theologian and scholar Romano Guardini, whose New Testament lectures she attended in Berlin and from whom she acquired a love of Kierkegaard and a lifelong interest in Christian theology that would inform some of her best writing and serve as a spiritual link with her future teachers Heidegger and Jaspers.

Hannah passed her university entrance exams a year ahead

of schedule. By the time she was ready to matriculate at the university in 1924, however, Beerwald could not afford to help her. The economic inflation that followed on the heels of the postwar recession proved ferociously destructive, promoting mass strikes, unemployment, and a wave of mergers that swallowed up small businesses and destroyed the old-fashioned, independent way of life of much of the nation's petit bourgeoisie. Like Eichmann at a slightly later date, Beerwald went to work for small wages as a traveling salesman.

At the last minute, an uncle by marriage on her father's side who still had money stepped forward to pay for the proud, promising young woman's university education. She was eighteen years old.

3

First Love

Heidegger in Marburg, 1924–1932

The hidden king reigned therefore in the realm of thinking.

— HANNAH ARENDT, "Heidegger at Eighty," 1971[1]

H ANNAH ARENDT'S ROMANCE with Anne Mendelssohn's cousin Ernst Grumach was brief. It stalled
when she left Königsberg for Berlin in 1922 and ended
when Grumach transferred from Albertina to Marburg University, near Frankfurt, in 1923. The young man had stumbled
upon the wildfire fame of a subversive professor of philosophy
named Martin Heidegger and had made a pilgrimage to study
with him. On Grumach's recommendation, Arendt did the
same. The consequences, both for her life and for the future of
"thinking," were large.

She entered Marburg, a sixteenth-century Protestant university, in the late fall of 1924 as a student of theology, philosophy, and classics. She immediately enrolled in Heidegger's lecture course, only his second at Marburg, called Basic Concepts
of Aristotelian Philosophy and in a smaller seminar whose cur-
riculum was a line-by-line appraisal in Greek of Plato's dialogue
Sophist. That class met in room 11 of the Old University Building on the hilltop campus overlooking the medieval town.[2] It
was while Heidegger was analyzing Being and Not Being in

Sophist that he first noticed the "great gaze" and "shivering soul" of the lovely teenager and decided, apparently on the spot, that he must have her.[3]

Heidegger was thirty-five years old and, although slight in stature, was romantic, brooding, and electrifying as both a thinker and a teacher. A former Catholic seminary student from a five-hundred-year-old woodland peasant family, he dressed idiosyncratically in knickerbockers, peasant smocks, and wide-lapelled Black Forest coats to express his passion for the preindustrial landscapes and folkways of his childhood home in rural Messkirch, in the Swabian Alps.[4] Like other neo-Romantics of the time, he loathed the intensifying industrialism and commercialism of his homeland after World War I. He was athletic. In winter, he could be seen striding toward the nearby Lahn hills carrying skis and wearing goggles.[5] Students called him "the little magician from Messkirch."

Heidegger had come to Marburg the previous year from the University of Freiburg, where he had been the rising understudy of a leading existentialist philosopher named Edmund Husserl; and although it would take Heidegger until 1927 to complete and publish *Sein und Zeit* (*Being and Time*), the masterwork of existential "phenomenology" that lifted him into the ranks of the century's great thinkers overnight, he was already the subject of widespread "rumors" and "murmurs," including handwritten notes circulated throughout the network of German universities by students stunned at the depth of his insights and the originality and fervor of his thought.[6] His lifelong subject was the nature of "what is" and "why," and his rallying cry was to rethink everything, from Plato and Aristotle to the classroom lectern from which he spoke and which once, in a memorable demonstration, he figuratively deconstructed into a series of wooden boxes that disappeared, metaphysically speaking, before his students' eyes.[7] He knew how to dazzle. "The rumor about Heidegger put it quite simply," Arendt wrote in 1969.

"Thinking has come to life again."[8] Her classmate Hans-Georg Gadamer declared that just "a glimpse of his eyes [and] one knew who he was and is: a visionary. A thinker who sees" and "made us see."[9] The technique of his lectures, which ranged at Marburg from Basic Concepts of Ancient Philosophy to Phenomenological Research,[10] involved building up "a complex structure of ideas," recalled another classmate, Karl Löwith, "which he then dismantled to confront the overstrung student with a puzzle and leave him in a void." Sometimes this "art of witchcraft," as Löwith called it, entailed risky results: "One student took her own life after three years of puzzle-solving."[11] For Arendt and a number of other highly attuned young scholars, his technique was deeply illuminating and immensely constructive. The teacher's approach to the mysterious problem of Being—that is, the universal Is that lies beneath all that is real, from puddles and stones to insects and numbers, and is strung like a tarpaulin over Nothingness—showed her that thinking was a passionate calling and, at times, a life-or-death struggle in pursuit of solid ground. Although Heidegger scheduled his lectures for as early as at seven in the morning,[12] he soon had 150 students attending, including many worshipful and willing young women.[13]

Arendt also drew attention during her first and only full academic year at Marburg. At age eighteen, she was spiritually intense, personally exotic, and both self-assured and shy. Having decided to study philosophy with a specialty in New Testament theology,[14] which also had been Heidegger's original field of study, she had prepared in Berlin by taking advanced Greek and Latin as well as auditing lectures by Guardini.[15] One of her early admirers, the improbably named Benno Georg Leopold von Wiese und Kaiserwaldau, a student of German language and literature with whom she had a brief affair in 1927,[16] wrote, "The most striking thing about her was the suggestive force that emanated from her eyes. One virtually drowned in them and feared never to come up again."[17] She wore her dark hair drawn back in a loose bun and a flattering green dress that fellow students could still recall years later. Hermann Mörchen, a future Heidegger specialist, remembered that conversations at surrounding tables in the dining hall would stop when Arendt spoke: Everyone wanted to hear her.[18] In Heidegger's lectures, she met and impressed an astonishing array of young students and scholars, many of them Jews who later came to the United States: her lifelong friend Hans Jonas, who from 1955 to 1976 taught philosophy at the New School for Social Research in New York City; Leo Strauss, a professor of political theory at the University of Chicago and a favored thinker among 1950s and 1960s neoconservatives, including Paul Wolfowitz; Herbert Marcuse, author of *Escape from Freedom* and a reluctant hero of the American New Left; the philosopher Karl Löwith; Hans-Georg Gadamer, author of *Truth and Method*; and Arendt's future first husband, the journalist and antinuclear activist Günther Stern, later known as Günther Anders.[19] Many of these men, including Strauss — whose University of Chicago classroom was down the hall from Arendt's but who, after *Eichmann,* reportedly refused to speak to her[20] — fell in love with her. Some became her devoted friends. As often happened in Arendt's life, there were few women outstanding enough to compete with her for attention, and she avoided Heidegger's male and female idolaters, of whom there were many.

Marburg was a provincial town of a few thousand people, dominated by the university, its students, and its faculty. Social life was sparse; gossip was rife. Heidegger was married. His wife, Elfride Petri, a practicing Lutheran and a former student of economics at Freiburg, where she and Heidegger had met, possessed a watchful nature and a steely will; Arendt later characterized her as "half-crazed" with jealousy, stupidity, and resentment.[21] In the mid-1920s, while her husband secretly pursued young Hannah, Elfride was reading Hitler's *Mein Kampf* and imbibing its vitriol and warlike aspirations. The couple had two sons.

Heidegger, too, was an anti-Semite, although an abstracted, pacific, and probably—given the time and place—unexceptional one, as Arendt would insist until her dying day. There was much she didn't know. He kept his most disturbing ideas about the specific vices of "world Jewry"—its invention of "homelessness" and "rootlessness," its penchant for the "empty rationality" and science of calculation that defines the modern world[22] — out of public view, contained in private notebooks and, beginning in the late 1920s, in letters to government officials,[23] whom he hoped to influence or even recruit to a new philosophical movement based on pre-Socratic modes of thinking.[24] His "Black Notebooks," so called because of the color of their bindings, have only recently been published, and only in German, and much of his official correspondence remains unpublished, in archives. But there were public displays of anti-Semitism Arendt did come to know about, including the fact of Heidegger's Nazi Party membership, beginning in 1933 and continuing until 1945, and his faithful and even enthusiastic service to the Nazi Party as a university rector and public speaker in the early 1930s.

He waited until February 1925 to make an overture to Arendt. It took the form of a letter. "Dear Miss Arendt!" it read. "I must come see you this evening and speak to your heart. Everything should be simple and clear and pure between us. . . . I will never be able to call you mine, but from now on you will belong in my life, and it shall grow with you."[25] Her answer is lost, as are most of her letters from this period, but she did not hesitate for long. A few days later he wrote to her again, exclaiming, "Dear Hannah! Why is love rich beyond all other possible human experiences and a sweet burden to those seized in its grasp?"[26] And shortly after that: "The demonic struck me. The silent prayer of your beloved hands and your shining brow enveloped it in womanly transfiguration. Nothing like it has ever happened to me."[27]

That nothing like this had happened to Heidegger is likely. During the Nazi years, he would confess to the unforgiving Elfride that Arendt had been "the passion of his life."[28] Although he would have other mistresses, Arendt was apparently the first and by far the most cherished, in part because she thoroughly understood his notoriously intricate and labored reasoning. In the small, jealous world of German academic philosophy in which he was pursuing fame, public exposure of a married professor's sexual affair with a first-year student would be disastrous, even if she weren't Jewish. He was risking a good deal for Arendt, and she knew it. She was risking at least as much for him.

The affair lasted three years. Heidegger decided when they saw each other. As long as she remained at Marburg, they met in her attic bed- and sitting room or in his office. "Please come *Friday* evening, like last time," he wrote.[29] He devised signals that she abided by. "If the lamp is lit in my room, I will have been detained by a meeting," in which case she was to "come again on Wednesday evening." He indicated what pleased him. (Her murmured "If you want to have me" and "If you like" left him moved for days, he wrote, as did her "shy quiet 'yes'" at the train station.") He praised her modesty and cherished her "pure brow." He tried to please her, too. He expressed longing for her company and gratitude for displays of love, encouraged her in her studies, read the poems she wrote and the poems she recommended, and wrote poems to her, sometimes in Greek. Secrecy was central. "Destroy this note!" he commanded in one letter.[30]

On the whole, he knew that he could count on her discretion. As with her father's illness, although for different reasons, she spoke of the affair to no one other than Anne Mendelssohn, Hans Jonas, Heinrich Blücher, and, after the war, Karl Jaspers. The sexual component of her relationship with Heidegger was not otherwise discovered until nearly a decade after both had died, within months of each other. The revelation caused a scandal, and the debate about it, particularly in view of Heidegger's Nazi history and her perspective on the Eichmann trial, continues, at times hysterically, to this day, helped along by Margarethe von Trotta's 2013 film *Hannah Arendt* and the 2014 publication in Germany of Heidegger's Black Notebooks.

In April 1925, Arendt returned home to Königsberg for spring vacation and composed "The Shadows." In this brief self-portrait, the matters most at stake for her in childhood and in her relationship with Heidegger become clear. The essay is dense, "poetic," a wistful confession of an eighteen-year-old girl pausing on the threshold of adulthood, afraid to give up the old "vague pain" and dreamy self-absorption that accompanies her familiar condition of being "ostracized" in exchange for a "pale and colorless" adulthood into which she fears the spell of the larger world will draw her. She ponders the disturbance she still feels from what she refers to, enigmatically, as "her helpless, betrayed youth." She hopes for release from "sickness and confusion" and from "fear of reality." She longs for clarity, simplicity, patience, and "organic growth," a Heideggerian phrase. She confesses, startlingly, that she expects the opposite: to live her life in "idle experiments and curiosity without rights or foundation," until "finally the long and eagerly awaited end takes her unawares, putting an arbitrary stop to her useless activity,"[31] the troubling premonition — wrong on every count except the suddenness of death — that ends the essay.

The mood of "The Shadows," if not its echoes of a painful and yet internally rich upbringing, is mysterious. Arendt certainly didn't regard herself as her classmates saw her: brilliant, lovely, vibrant, self-possessed, and immensely promising. The writing is abstract, without a single specific recollection to explain her pessimism and despair — a foreshadowing, some might say, of her often difficult adult style. She gives no hint that she was writing to a brand-new lover, let alone to Heidegger: no elation, no flirtation, no effort to impress—except, perhaps, by what she doesn't reveal about her childhood and by her self-conscious tone of "authenticity," a favorite constituent of Heideggerian thought and of neo-Romantic movements everywhere. She doesn't seek approval. If anything, she seems to be warning Heidegger that she has no "foundation" in the world, no platform from which to meet his passionate conviction of being rooted in the German soil and German folkways. The idea—for Arendt, still only a notion—that having a "foundation" of some kind confers "rights" is one she would consider in depth and to powerful effect in her essays of the 1940s and in *The Origins of Totalitarianism,* but here she may simply be reflecting the mythology of the philosopher himself, who wished to "open [himself] up to the vastness of the sky and at the same time be rooted in the dark of the earth."[32] She was already an outsider, standing apart, unrooted. She doesn't mention her Jewishness, nor does he; but her willingness to live without "foundation" and her refusal to deceive herself are primary qualities of the budding, self-defined, and proud pariah Hannah Arendt would become.

She gave "The Shadows" to her lover in late April 1925. His response was immediate and on the surface reassuring. "There are 'shadows' only where there is *sun*," he wrote, perhaps thinking of Plato's allegory of the cave; and the sun, which represents the "good" in Plato, "is the foundation of your soul," he added. But he also expressed alarm, even disdain, and an admonishment: "I would not love you if I were not convinced that those shadows are not *you* but distortions and illusions produced by an endless self-erosion that penetrated from outside." Nevertheless, he warned, "the way out of such existential contortions, which are not really yours, will be long." Given what is now known about Heidegger's anti-Semitism, it is hard not to read this passage as both a promise to overlook her Jewishness and an implied threat should its "shadows" overtake her.

Back at the university for the summer semester, Arendt enrolled in Heidegger's seminar on Descartes's *Meditations* and his now legendary lecture course History of the Concept of Time. She resumed her evening meetings with her lover, who began coaxing her to be a "happy," "good," "confident," "sparkling," "free," and self-sufficient girl, bringing "sunshine" and "helpful joy" into his life. Whether she considered his prompting well intended, self-serving, or a not very subtle reminder of his warning about the conditional nature of his love, she did her best, and he frequently complimented her on her progress toward the light.

Meanwhile, the clouds were gathering over Germany. By 1925, Hitler, who was jailed for sedition in 1924, was newly freed and traveling the region, recruiting true believers to the Nazi Party and drawing crowds with vicious anti-Marxist, anti-Jewish speeches. Three years earlier, he had founded the Sturmabteilung (SA) — the predecessor of the SS to which Eichmann belonged — and the Nazi Youth movement, both of which were gaining membership. Hans Jonas recalled a Marburg fraternity boy wearing a National Socialist uniform who tried to seat himself beside Arendt in a student restaurant; she was so frightened that Jonas intervened. Applying in person to take a seminar on the "anthropology" of the apostle Paul with the New Testament theologian Rudolf Bultmann, she let Bultmann know that "there must be no anti-Semitic remarks" in class.[33] Like her mother, he assured her that if there were, he and she would handle them together. In July, Hitler published the first of two best-selling volumes of *Mein Kampf.* Anti-Semitism was closing in.

Gradually, Heidegger's ardor lessened. In late May 1925, he was too busy to meet with Arendt. In June, before leaving Marburg for an extended retreat to a mountain cabin that his wife, Elfride, had paid to have built as a refuge for him in the Black Forest town of Todtnauberg, he reminded Arendt that they must practice "a love strong for the future, and not just a moment's fleeting pleasure."[34] His letters from Todtnauberg brim with descriptions of woodland hikes, Alpine views, and work well done on the final draft of *Being and Time,* and often express reluctance to return. "I am dreading the semester" to come, he wrote, because it will "tear me away from the really productive work." When they both returned to campus in late October 1925, his letters were frankly plaintive, and he took to mentioning his wife and children, who were ill with colds and flu.

Arendt attended every class he gave, including a seminar called Phenomenological Exercises for Advanced Students, in which she read Kant and Hegel.[35] But in her few surviving poems of the period, she pondered his apparent distance from her, writing in one, "Why is the giving of your hand so secret and so shy? And you from so far a land you do not know our wine?" Work came first for him, of course. But he seemed now to be consigning her to the ordinary background of his life, where all the prosaic distractions lay and where she had no "foundation" and no "rights." "Come with me and be my love," she urged in the same poem.[36] She was already far beyond him in the courage to be unconventional, but still felt keenly the pangs brought on by his diminishing attention.

That fall, Heidegger was preparing *Being and Time* for approval by his mentor and friend Edmund Husserl and for delivery to the printer by April 1926.[37] His appointment to a full professorship depended on meeting the deadline. In early January, he forgot an evening engagement with Arendt that he had requested only the day before. "I forgot you —" he wrote, "not from indifference, not because external circumstances intruded between us, but because I had to forget and will forget you whenever I withdraw into the final stages of my work." He referred to their "friendship" and added, "I know that I will draw you back to me again."[38]

He would — but not then. Arendt, practiced at separation, had had enough. She decided to leave Marburg. ("I left Marburg exclusively for your sake," she wrote to him twenty-five years later.)[39] From hints in earlier letters, they seem to have discussed this possibility in advance; he may even have pressured her to go, as Elzbieta Ettinger, who first discovered the details of the love affair in 1995, suggested in her book *Hannah Arendt/ Martin Heidegger.* Both were aware that the danger of exposure intensified as their meetings continued; Elfride was pointedly rude to Arendt when they met, and the approaching publication of his book made Heidegger not merely a rumor but also an object of rumors. Within the year, Arendt was supposed to begin research for her doctoral dissertation, which she could not honorably do under the patronage of Heidegger. Finally, as deeply within his thrall as she was, she would not let him set the terms of her exile. Her letter to him, which is lost, contained a drop of acid. Recalling some jesting that she and friends had engaged in over the outsized egos of "philosophers," she lured Heidegger to take the bait: "Only a fool or a bureaucrat would condemn such [jokes]," he sniffed. But he knew what she didn't: He planned to maintain his hold on her after she was at a safe remove.

The end of Arendt's third semester, in April 1926, brought to a close the first, most intimate stage of her love affair with the man she later referred to not only as the "hidden king" of thinking but also, after World War II, as a "liar" and a "fox."[40] Although she had other love affairs in 1927 and 1928, including with the aristocratic Benno von Wiese, who himself later joined the Nazi Party, and a forty-year-old expressionist writer named Erwin Loewenson, Heidegger persuaded her to continue their clandestine meetings — always at his instigation and typically in small towns along convenient railway routes. *Being and Time* brought him international acclaim in 1927. Then, in April 1928, Heidegger's friend Husserl, retiring from his chairmanship in philosophy at the University of Freiburg,[41] recommended the younger man to take his place. It was a visible promotion.

Arendt, now too dangerous, too inconvenient, or possibly too Jewish for his new prominence, had to be dealt with. That month, he abruptly ended this second, intermittent phase of the affair.

He broke the news to her in Heidelberg, where she was completing her doctoral dissertation on Saint Augustine's concept of love under the direction of Heidegger's colleague the avuncular Karl Jaspers. Arendt and Heidegger "reunited" (Arendt's term) on an evening in late April; the next day, he canceled a second meeting. Nonetheless, Arendt wrote him a farewell message. "So you aren't coming now — I think I understand," she offered. "But I still have been . . . overcome by an almost bafflingly urgent fear," presumably the old fear of being abandoned by a man who was at least in part a father figure to her. "I love you as I did on the first day," she told him. She added, "I would lose my right to live if I lost my love for you, but I would lose this love and its *reality* if I shirked the responsibility it forces on me." The references to "reality" and "responsibility" are important, for Arendt already knew that her road was "wide and not a leap, [and] runs through the world." The *leap* — Heidegger's word for a spiritual flight beyond the limits of time and history, which the philosopher prided himself on taking — was not for her. Unlike him, she sensed that she would thrash her way through a thicket of duties, desires, and political exigencies. She said goodbye with a quotation from Elizabeth Barrett Browning's *Sonnets from the Portuguese,* translated into German by Rainer Maria Rilke: "And, if God choose, I shall but love thee better after death."[42] This was not a threat of suicide, as a few writers have suggested, but a promise that their paths would cross again in another time and place, as — considering World War II as a kind of cultural death — indeed they would.

She saw Heidegger once more before she fled Germany in 1933. In February 1929, she moved in with Günther Stern, another former Heidegger student[43] whom both Heidegger and

his wife despised — Elfride because Stern was a Jew and Heidegger because the younger man had once parroted the philosopher's ideas as if they were his own. "Mr. Stern is . . . one of the
worst" of the students who depleted his energy, Heidegger had
written to Arendt in 1925.[44] Now, three and a half years later,
she wrote to him: "I have found a home and a sense of belonging with someone"— Stern —"about whom you might understand it least of all."[45] She married Stern in September 1929,
with her mother and the elder Sterns proudly in attendance. A
few days later, Heidegger paid the newlyweds a visit — perhaps
to gauge whether his affair with her could be rekindled, as it had
been in 1927. When it was time for Heidegger to leave, Arendt
accompanied him and Stern to the railway station, from which
they both happened to be taking the same train. Absorbed in
conversation with each other, the men did not wave good-bye
to Arendt. Stern's absentmindedness seems not to have both-
ered her. But later that day, she wrote to Heidegger about the
"diabolical clarity" with which she saw how easily he forgot her.
He had looked through the railway carriage window, she wrote,
looked away, then looked back again and had seen but not *recognized* her; she was anxiously reminded of an episode from early
childhood in which Martha, acting out the story line of a fairy
tale, pretended not to know her because her nose had grown. "I
kept crying: but I am your child, I am your Hannah. — That's
what it was like today," she wrote.[46] That this memory was set at
a time when her father, in the final stages of syphilis, could no
longer recognize *his* child adds a stab of poignancy to the young
woman's last glimpse of her lover for the next twenty years.

Günther Stern was the only son of two prominent and
thoroughly assimilated child psychologists, William and Clara
Stern. In 1930, he tried out for what was called an academic
"habilitation," or advanced doctoral degree and university appointment, but failed to win faculty backing. Arendt's marriage to him lasted for a few years and then dissolved in incom-

patibility. By the mid-1930s, when they were living together in Paris, the "home" she had hoped to find with him had become a "hell," she wrote to her soon-to-be second husband, Heinrich Blücher.[47] She was immensely more successful than Stern — or Blücher, for that matter. She published her dissertation on Saint Augustine in 1929 and, with the support of a paid fellowship, completed all but two chapters of a richly autobiographical study of the life of a gifted eighteenth-century "Jewess" named Rahel Varnhagen, which was intended to be her own "habilitation" thesis, before the passage of the first of Hitler's anti-Jewish employment laws made a university career an impossible ambition for her and many others.

The portrait of Varnhagen, begun as a study of high German Romanticism in 1929, completed in Paris in 1938, and published as *Rahel Varnhagen: The Life of a Jewess* in 1957,[48] marked a turning point for Arendt. By 1930, she was aware that "the Nazis were our enemies," as she told Günter Gaus in 1964, and that "a large number of the German people were behind them." "That had been completely evident for at least four years" before Hitler assumed power in 1933 "to everyone who wasn't feebleminded," she said.[49] Studying the life and letters of Varnhagen, among the first wave of Prussian Jews to assimilate into German haute bourgeois society after the Jewish Enlightenment, was Arendt's early attempt to pierce the "Jewish Question," which she had heard debates about all her life but only now found compelling. She called Varnhagen "my very closest woman friend, [although] unfortunately dead one hundred years now,"[50] and told Gaus, "I wrote with the idea, 'I want to understand.'"[51]

Rahel, born Rahel Levin into a wealthy merchant family in 1771, bitterly hated the fact of her "infamous birth," her "disgrace," as a Jew.[52] Like Paul and Martha, who were of an age to have been Rahel's great-great-grandchildren, Rahel embraced social and cultural assimilation in her time. She availed herself of Berlin's new fashion in the late eighteenth century for "ex-

ception Jews"—men and women set apart from the mass of
Jews by virtue of wealth, scholarship, artistic talent, or connec-
tions—by creating and hosting one of the most celebrated literary salons of her day, attended by French and German poets,
politicians, diplomats, and stylish young aristocrats. She had affairs with some of these, including Count Karl-Wilhelm Finck
von Finckenstein, the son and grandson of Prussian field mar-
shals, whom she plotted to marry; to her sorrow, he refused to
make a permanent alliance with her. ("How wretched it is always to have to legitimize myself!" Arendt quotes Rahel as writing to a friend. "That is why it is so disgusting to be a Jew.") At
age forty, she converted to Christianity and married a Prussian
diplomat named Karl August Varnhagen von Ense, who was
devoted to her for the rest of her life. But this didn't solve her
problem: In Arendt's words it merely illustrated "all that a Jew
could undertake without ceasing to be a Jew." The price of full
assimilation—as Arendt discovered through the experience of
Varnhagen, as recorded in thousands of letters to friends—was
to turn against oneself, to internalize "that invigorating sport of
good society, the 'modern hatred of Jews.'" In an environment
fundamentally hostile to Jews, which included "all countries in
which Jews lived, down to the twentieth century," Arendt wrote
toward the end of *Rahel Varnhagen,* "it is possible to assimilate
only by assimilating to anti-Semitism also,"[53] making one a hyp-
ocrite and a "scoundrel." That Varnhagen would not do. Neither would Arendt.

Living vicariously with Varnhagen marked the end of
Arendt's period of spiritual timidity—that "vague pain" or
"dreamy, spellbound sense of being ostracized"—and the beginning of social and political fervor. It was while reading Varnhagen's letters and diaries that she first made her well-known distinction between the "parvenu" and the "conscious pariah" in
Jewish life and, indeed, in all times and cultures; between those
who attempt to compensate for an enforced sense of social infe-

riority by striving to become aristocrats, magnates, or stars — in other words, special exceptions by virtue of a special gift — and those who affirm and find strength in their identity as enlightened outsiders, as Varnhagen did in her old age.[54] Arendt began her study of Varnhagen by quoting the Jewess on her deathbed in 1833, as recorded by her husband: "What a history!" the old woman declared. "A fugitive from Egypt and Palestine, here I am.... The thing which all my life seemed to me the greatest shame, which was the misery and misfortune of my life — having been born a Jewess — this I would on no account now wish to have missed." "I am a rebel after all!" she exclaimed elsewhere in her letters. In adopting this distinction between the parvenu, who aspires to the social status of her political adversaries, and the pariah, an independent spirit who refuses to wear a mask or climb a ladder, Arendt discovered her own stance for the next decade of her life and, in some respects, the basis of her character.

Varnhagen became a rebel because she refused to lie to herself. In 1931 and 1932, Arendt received reports that Heidegger, who now directed the philosophy department at Freiburg, had taken to excluding Jews from his seminars and snubbing them in public. She wrote to him, expressing shock and anger. He answered, petulantly, listing the Jewish students he had helped who either didn't deserve his help or hadn't thanked him for it and bewailing the eternal slanders against him. "Whoever wants to call that [my help] 'raging anti-Semitism' is welcome to do so," he complained, adding, "[I]t cannot touch my relationship with you."[55] In April 1933, three months after Hitler came to power, Heidegger was elected — or, more accurately, elevated in a coup by right-leaning faculty members — to be Freiburg's rector, or president.[56] A week later, he joined the Nazi Party. In April 1934, disaffected because of his lack of influence or importance among the Nazis, he retreated to teaching but did not resign his party membership. Until war's end, he behaved much as Arendt had heard, handing off his Jewish students to other professors and avoiding Jewish colleagues, who gradually disappeared into permanent exile or concentration camps. About this, Heidegger said nothing, then or at any time until his death in 1976. He disparaged his benefactor Edmund Husserl, who, a Jew by birth although a Lutheran convert, was soon stripped of his privileges as an emeritus professor and died in 1938 of pleurisy and, so Arendt believed, a broken heart. ("I can't but regard Heidegger as a potential murderer," she wrote to Karl Jaspers about this episode in 1946.)[57] As rector, Heidegger delivered public speeches about German "authenticity" indwelling in the "nature, history, language, the *Volk,* custom, the state" of Germany,[58] and throughout the 1930s he privately enlarged the concept of Being to include the notion that Being in the world, a core element of his thinking, means to be rooted in the soil of a nation, to which some people belong by virtue of ancestry and language and others do not.[59] In her mature work, Arendt fiercely affirmed that being alive means being *somewhere.* But by then she well understood the menace of "peoples" and nation-states founded on "blood and soil."

The influence of Heidegger on Arendt is hard to overestimate. His teaching deepened her love of rich philosophic and poetic language, words fished from the depths of etymology to express ideas for which there are no adequate conventional descriptions. She believed, with him, that authentic truths arise only "out of an ultimate and absolute precision in the use of words," as she noted in *Rahel Varnhagen*[60] and might also have written in *Eichmann,* for she could not take seriously a "clown" in a cage who contradicted himself and did not speak well. "The longer one listened to him [Eichmann], the more obvious it became that his inability to speak" in anything other than repetitive clichés "was closely connected to his inability to *think.*"[61] This is pure Heidegger, who wrote about "thoughtlessness" as "the endless chattering and calculation of modernity that always destroys deep, authentic thought,"[62] and may also have been a serious misreading of Eichmann.

Early in their affair, soon after reading "The Shadows," Heidegger wrote to her, *"Amo* means *volo, ut sis,* [as] Augustine once said." He translated this as "I love you — I want you to be what you are."[63] She repeated this saying all her life: in correspondence with Heinrich Blücher, in *The Origins of Totalitarianism*,[64] in her posthumously published book about thinking, *The Life of the Mind.* It may have contributed to her choice of Saint Augustine's concepts of love as a dissertation topic, which — with its focus on neighborly love — enriched her political thought with a profound belief in the potential of every human birth to effect change. Heidegger's recognition of her gifts and distinction, his passion both for her "dear figure" and her "innermost essence," his acknowledged wish to draw her close to him in preference to the more conventional young women clamoring for his attention — all of this built her confidence, which was at a low point in "The Shadows." The writer Elzbieta Ettinger went further, claiming that Arendt "shared the insecurity of many assimilated Jews who were still uncertain about their place." By choosing her as his beloved, Ettinger wrote, "Heidegger fulfilled for Hannah the dream of generations of German Jews, going back to such pioneers as Rahel Varnhagen."[65] In some respects, at least, he fortified her strengths — she *was* exceptional — and prepared her to embrace, find language for, and defend all of who she was.

Along with Varnhagen and the raw force of German history, Heidegger also awakened her from the dream of assimilation. His turning toward the Nazis, irrefutable after 1933, was a blunt shock and a wound. "The problem, the personal problem, was not what our enemies did but what our friends did," she said to Gaus in 1964,[66] and one can sense sadness in the simplicity of the statement. Her critics — including Ettinger — have often argued that the affair with Heidegger represented a form of Jewish "self-hatred," which they find abundantly expressed in *Eichmann*. That she, at the height of her own fame, gave every appearance of having forgiven him was held against her as a sign of divided loyalty, at best.

She was much less moderate in 1933, when she learned of his official speeches and administrative actions on behalf of Hitler. Her revulsion for Heidegger and others like him led her to renounce her formal studies. "I lived in an intellectual milieu," she recalled in 1964. "And among intellectuals *Gleichschaltung* [voluntary cooperation with the Nazis] was the rule, so to speak. But not among the others. . . . I left Germany dominated by the idea — of course somewhat exaggerated: Never again! . . . I want nothing to do with that [intellectual] lot."[67] For years afterward, in Paris and New York City, she sought out the company of artists, writers, and political activists rather than academicians and obtained practical work as an organizational aide to Zionist and Jewish agencies and projects. "If one is attacked as a Jew, one must defend oneself as a Jew," she said — offering the rallying cry of both the pariah and the incipient political theorist in Hannah Arendt.

4

We Refugees
Berlin and Paris in the 1930s

All the vaunted Jewish qualities — the "Jewish heart,"
humanity, humor, disinterested intelligence — are
pariah qualities. All Jewish shortcomings — tactlessness,
political stupidity, inferiority complexes and money-
grubbing — are characteristic of upstarts.

— HANNAH ARENDT, "We Refugees," 1943[1]

HAVING DECIDED NOT to be an intellectual,
Arendt became an outlaw.
        In February 1933, a month after Hitler was named
chancellor of Germany, the Reichstag building in Berlin was
set on fire. Blaming the Communists, Hitler took the occa-
sion to suspend civil liberties and order mass arrests of Communists and other Nazi Party adversaries. Günther Stern, who had
friends and associates on the Communist Left, including Bertolt Brecht, in whose address book his name appeared, fled with
his friends to Paris. Arendt stayed behind, determined to resist
Nazi intimidation for as long as she was able: "One [couldn't]
simply be a bystander!" she later said.[2] Fully aware of the threat
to her safety, "she was equipped for resistance with a splendid
impertinence," a friend from that period remarked.[3]
        She was arrested several weeks later, on her way to meet

her mother for lunch at a café in Berlin, where she and Stern had been living since the fall of 1931. In the hectic and fearful months leading up to Nazi seizure of power, she had renewed her friendship with Kurt Blumenfeld, Max's friend, now fifty years old and the director of the Zionist Federation of Germany. With Stern in Paris, she offered their Berlin apartment as a way station for fleeing Jewish activists, Communists, and others who had to leave Germany quickly. Martha, a few friends from Königsberg and Freiburg, and assorted others came to visit, creating a daily commotion that served to disguise the illegal comings and goings of the fugitives; and Arendt's social circle filled up with Zionist activists, including Blumenfeld, the philosopher Martin Buber, and the publisher Salman Schocken.

With spring came a Nazi boycott of Jewish shops and businesses and the first wave of laws restricting Jewish liberties. Blumenfeld asked Arendt to pay clandestine visits to the Prussian State Library, where she had done her research on Varnhagen, and copy passages from newspapers and journals showing the intensity of anti-Jewish animus among ordinary Germans, including members of trade associations and social clubs. Blumenfeld planned to use this material in a speech to the Eighteenth Zionist Congress in Prague the following summer, with the aim of rousing still-optimistic German Jewish leaders into a sense of collective urgency and action. The time had come to renounce assimilation, proclaim unity, and organize to emigrate, preferably to Palestine, he argued. For the most part, Arendt agreed. She had known for months that she would be forced to leave. "Jews could not stay," she recalled in 1964. "I did not intend to run around Germany as a second-class citizen," later adding, "[The Zionists] were the only ones who were ready."[4]

She was pleased with Blumenfeld's assignment, although it was now illegal to collect or disseminate what the Nazis called "horror propaganda" against their anti-Jewish policy. The task gave her a feeling "that something could be done after all," she later said. Apparently she was being spied on, however, for after a few weeks of shuttling back and forth to the library, she was intercepted by an officer from one of Hitler's new political units—"a charming fellow"—who politely escorted her to the central Berlin police station. She remained there, feigning innocence, while officials searched her apartment, confiscated her notebooks, and brought her mother in for questioning. Martha admitted nothing, and the notebooks were in code: Arendt had made notes using ancient Greek characters, which the storm troopers could no more decipher than Hebrew or Japanese. Still, she was held for eight days and might have disappeared into one of the new "Gestapo cellars" or concentration camps, except that her arresting officer, who was young, new to his job, and probably smitten with twenty-six-year-old Hannah, arranged for her release, presumably to be followed by a judicial hearing.[5]

Arendt didn't wait. She and Martha packed a suitcase and left Germany, Arendt traveling without a passport, an exit visa, or any legal papers. They took the refugees' grapevine-recommended route, through the forested Erzgebirge Mountains between Germany and Czechoslovakia into Prague, by train to Geneva, and finally, in the fall of 1933, to Paris and reunion with Günther Stern. Martha, who had both papers and permission to travel, returned to Königsberg and her husband, Martin Beerwald.

Arendt found Stern in a depressed mood, unable to find a steady means to earn a living, a circumstance shared by almost every German émigré they knew. He was writing an immense, dark, dystopian satire of fascist tyranny called "The Molussian Catacombs" (never published but adapted by French filmmaker Nicolas Rey in 2012). Arendt, in contrast, was full of purpose, if not yet fully aware of the precariousness of her stateless situation. In Geneva, she had made a decision to align herself with "the Jewish cause," she later said, to do "exclusively and only

Jewish work." She began there by working as an aide to a friend of Martha's at the League of Nations' Jewish Agency for Palestine, helping to distribute entry visas to Jewish settlers and writing speeches.

In Paris, she polished her clerical skills and found a job as a secretary for a Zionist-funded outreach program called Agriculture et Artisanat, which trained young Jewish refugees for lives as farmers and craftsmen in the experimental villages and communes of Palestine. One of her duties was to coordinate evening lectures in Jewish history, Hebrew, and Zionism for her student charges. While she immersed herself in French she also studied Hebrew. "I want to know my own people," she told her Hebrew tutor, a Polish refugee named Chanan Klenbort. She even learned some Yiddish: "the only German Jew far and wide" to have done so, she claimed.[6] She was promoted to office manager and was able to support herself and Stern until the organization closed in 1935.

Although she certainly wouldn't always consider herself a mainstream Zionist, the "Jewish Question," which she had earlier found irrelevant, "became a personal fate" when she immigrated to Paris. "[B]elonging to Judaism had become my own problem, and my own problem was political."[7]

Paris was filled with German Jewish and central European refugees in the mid-1930s, many, like Arendt, living in the cheaper hotels and rooming houses of the Latin Quarter. Her marriage to Stern quickly became cool and often discordant, but they maintained a social life together and spent their odd hours in Left Bank cafés, talking with Anne Mendelssohn, who was also living in Paris, and Stern's friends Arnold Zweig[8] and Bertolt Brecht,[9] who was already famous for *The Threepenny Opera* and *Rise and Fall of the City of Mahagonny*. Notwithstanding his decades-long Stalinism and what the English historian Paul Johnson called his "heart of ice,"[10] Arendt henceforth defended Brecht as the greatest German poet of her lifetime,[11] invoking both Plato and Goethe in extenuation of his flaws of character. She also renewed a passionate intellectual friendship with the literary critic Walter Benjamin, a distant relative of Stern's who, although in fragile health and often subject to despair, taught her to love walking the streets of Paris. She met but wasn't impressed by Jean-Paul Sartre, then in his twenties and working on the novel *Nausea*. A decade later, as the celebrated author of *Being and Nothingness* (1943), he would follow in Heidegger's footsteps as the nearly universal idol of a new generation of philosophic-minded youth.

In some manner lost to history, Arendt also made the acquaintance of the Baroness Germaine de Rothschild, the wife of the fantastically rich Édouard Alphonse James de Rothschild of the French wing of the Rothschild bank. When her work at Agriculture et Artisanat ended in 1935, the baroness hired her to advise the family on the relative merits of the Jewish charities they supported or were being asked to support, including synagogues, schools, a seminary, religious courts of law, kosher businesses, and social welfare agencies. During the few months Arendt worked for her, she observed with keen interest the family's public exhibitions of social privilege and material splendor — as well as their unwitting displays of an ancient aversion to politics that kept them and their fellow "notables"[12] and social parvenus at a safe remove from government policy, except where their financial interests were concerned, and made them hesitant to offer support to the wave of so-called Ostjuden making its way to France. They worried that the newcomers' poverty, religiosity, and illiteracy in French and other European languages might further awaken the anti-Semites of France, who were irritably stirring in sympathy with Hitler.[13]

Arendt had heard this line of argument before as a child in Königsberg. She encountered it now with increasing impatience and a sense that it was self-defeating. She knew that, given the chance, Hitler's thugs would not exempt a Rothschild. "I realized what I then expressed time and again in the sentence: If one is attacked as a Jew, one must defend oneself as a Jew. Not as a German, not as a world citizen, not as an upholder of the Rights of Man."[14] She was prescient. When Germany invaded France in 1940, Germaine and Édouard de Rothschild and their youngest daughter, Bethsabée, temporarily deprived of their riches, were forced to flee for their lives by exactly the same hazardous route that Arendt and many others took.

In 1935 Arendt began a new job as director of the Paris branch of a Zionist children's emergency resettlement agency called Youth Aliyah.[15] Late that year, she led a group of refugee children from Marseilles to their new home in Palestine by ship, and for the first time she saw the spectacular mixed-ethnic cities of Syracuse, Haifa, Jerusalem, and Petra. She was fascinated by the Greek and Roman ruins she discovered among the Jewish, Arab, and Christian monuments and was moved by a sense of the enterprise, opportunities, and relative safety presented by earlier Jewish settlers to her group of desperate young émigrés. She admired the bold experiment in Jewish egalitarianism that the crafts villages and rural kibbutzim of Zion represented, some of which she visited with her cousin Ernst Fuerst, late of the Beerwaldian Greek Circle, and his young wife, Käthe Levin, who had moved to Jerusalem from Germany in 1934.[16] Later, both Fuersts and their daughter Edna Brocke would blame Heinrich Blücher for Arendt's criticism of Israel and animosity toward David Ben-Gurion.[17] "He hated Jews," said Edna Brocke, "though all his women were Jewish." But even in 1935 Arendt perceived that "one could not live" in the kibbutzim. "'Rule by your neighbors,' that is of course what it finally amounts to," she later wrote in a letter to Mary McCarthy.[18]

Arendt met Blücher at a public lecture in Paris one evening in the spring of 1936. By the time they met again, in June, she was separated from Günther Stern, who had left Paris for New York. The seven-year alliance with Stern was conclusively if unofficially over, and Arendt was relieved. "I wanted to dissolve my marriage three years ago," she wrote to Blücher from Geneva, where she and her Youth Aliyah colleagues were attending the first World Jewish Congress of August 1936. "My only option, I felt, was passive resistance, termination of all matrimonial duties. . . . I held on to my passive resistance with the same tenacity that he held on to the concept of being married to me."[19]

Blücher, in many ways the opposite of Stern, was a rough, charismatic charmer and "uncorruptible genius"[20] with whom Arendt fell immediately and permanently in love. He was not an obvious romantic choice for Paul and Martha's daughter, Heidegger's promising pupil, or even the active Zionist Arendt had recently become. Five-foot-four, barrel-chested,[21] far from handsome, garrulous, the only child of a German laundress and a factory worker who had been killed in an industrial accident before his birth, a Communist Party operative who was in hiding from both German officials and French and Russian thugs, he was sleeping on friends' couches and working at odd jobs when Arendt met him. A high school dropout, he was a voracious reader of difficult texts and had mastered much of German philosophy, art history, and political and military history on his own. If not exactly Christian, he was not Jewish and had no particular sympathy with the political aims of the Zionist movement. Like many on the European Left in the 1930s, he preferred that all of Hitler's foes to band together.[22] He was a natural rebel, more so than Arendt. After a brief stint in the German army in his late teens during World War I, where he was gassed — which may explain a lifetime of chronic lung and kidney ailments[23] — he joined the socialist Spartacist League, led by Martha's hero Rosa Luxemburg, whom Hannah also came greatly to admire and about whose common-law husband, Leo Jogiches, she later wrote, "He definitely was a man of action and passion, he knew how to do and how to suffer."[24] The same was true of Heinrich.

As a youth, Heinrich was active — and took pleasure at least as much as he suffered. He skirmished with the proto-Nazi Freikorps in the streets of Berlin during the 1919 Spartacist League Uprising—which must have impressed Hannah, if not her mother, who never warmed to the working-class, non-Jewish Heinrich. That same year he joined the German Communist Party, where his ten-year-long career as an organizer and propagandist involved a furtive trip to Soviet Russia and was risqué enough that he lied about it — and a number of other things — in conversation and on official documents for the remainder of his life. Like Stern and their shared acquaintance Bertolt Brecht, he fled Berlin, sans papers, a few days after the Reichstag fire. Even after he moved in with Hannah, he traveled the streets of Paris under an assumed name[25] and in the disguise of a member of the bourgeoisie: suit, hat, and walking stick, as though he were a well-heeled tourist or one of Walter Benjamin's flaneurs. He was "so illegal he didn't know where he lived," recalled his friend Charlotte Sempell, who sometimes gave him money.[26] He was a member of a Marxist discussion group that met in Benjamin's rented room. He referred to himself and Robert Gilbert,[27] a favorite sidekick, as "a couple of layabouts,"[28] a description that fit him for the next dozen years, to the grim satisfaction of Martha, who considered him lazy as well as rude.

Hannah Arendt didn't mind any of it. He wooed her with brainpower and native passion, employing scraps of poetry, political monologue, and sexual heat. Deeply enthralled, she was also reticent, as she had been with Heidegger. "And though you have forced me so very wonderfully, so very uncomfortably, to show trust, I show it only to you, only privately," she wrote to him in 1936. She wished they had met ten years earlier, for "in the meantime, unfortunately, I was forced to some extent to stop being a woman," presumably with Günther Stern. "I feel bad about that for your sake."[29] He was manly in reply. "Do not feel sorry for me because of the ten years etc. I am fully aware of what I have, and of what you are as a woman, and what you will be and will yet be — let me be the judge, for what can you know about these things."[30]

Apparently she confided in him — as in few others — the shattering history of Heidegger's multiple betrayals. She and Blücher were both married to others, he to a Lithuanian immigrant in Germany who had wanted a German passport and needed a German husband to get one. They moved in together in the late summer of 1936, filed for their divorces,[31] and were married in a civil ceremony on January 16, 1940. Thus began a thirty-year partnership that Arendt's New York friend Alfred Kazin described as "the most passionate seminar I would ever witness between a man and a woman living together" and the poet Randall Jarrell called a "Dual Monarchy" of intellectual geniuses who never stopped talking to each other about poetry, philosophy, and politics.

It would turn out that Blücher was a philanderer — like Heidegger, but without the manipulativeness or preening; and Arendt minded this not much more than she minded his not being Jewish, not being respectable, and not being held in high regard by Martha.[32] "Look, you yourself said 'everything speaks against it,'" she wrote to him early on. "What is this 'everything' — apart from prejudices and the difficulties and the petty fears — except that we might not have a world in common?"[33] Their common world was made up of an ardent, almost delirious love of conversation, disdain for much bourgeois convention, a shifting "tribe" of mutual friends, bedrock loyalty, and the certainty of being recognized, and it became their only reliable home for many years. She addressed him as Snubby, "my little tomcat," and "my beloved miracle rabbi," slyly referencing Marx. He called her simply "dearest." They were seekers together, far from home, traipsing shoulder to shoulder while "that old trickster, World-History,"[34] stole familiar landmarks from their path.

Martha met Heinrich for the first time in the spring of 1939. She arrived in Paris a few months after Kristallnacht, the terrifying night of anti-Jewish pillage and murder instigated by the Nazi Party after the assassination of a German consular officer in Paris by a young Polish Jew, whose father, as it happened, later testified at the Eichmann trial. During Kristallnacht in Königsberg, the Reform synagogue where Hannah's grandfather Max had worshipped was destroyed[35] and Hannah's paternal uncle by marriage Ernst Aron, who had helped to fund her education, died or was killed. Following on the German invasion of Austria in March 1938, the brutality of Kristallnacht that November changed "eloquent optimism" to "speechless pessimism" among German Jews, Hannah later wrote,[36] and Martha decided to join her daughter in France. It wasn't easy, as most remaining legal paths out of Germany were blocked for Jews. Heinrich sent his friend Charlotte Sempell, who was not only wealthy but also a Christian, to Königsberg to smooth Martha's passage. The women could not persuade the stolid Beerwald to join them, and he remained behind.

Arendt was helping to prepare Youth Aliyah for the wider hostilities everyone knew were coming. When England and France declared war on Germany in September 1939, her colleagues packed up the Paris office and moved to London. She rejoined the Paris branch of the Geneva-based Jewish Agency for Palestine, which was attempting to supply food and housing to the Jewish refugees arriving in Paris from occupied Austria and Czechoslovakia. But if the French had once been hospitable to Hitler's outcasts, they were not now. New restrictions were imposed, and panic and misery set in. "[O]nce we were somebodies about whom people cared," Arendt wrote of this period. "Once we could buy our food and ride on the subway without being told we were undesirable." By 1939, even some of those whose job it was to help found it hard to keep the refugees' humanity in view. "Herr Doktor, Herr Doktor, Herr Schnorrer,

Herr Schnorrer!" Arendt recalled hearing the director of a "great charity" in Paris—perhaps a Rothschild—exclaim upon receiving yet another letter from a German Jewish intellectual who needed aid, as she bitterly recorded in an essay called "We Refugees" in 1943.[37]

That fall, France ordered Blücher, who fell into the category of a German male national with a questionable political record, into an interment camp in southern France. He spent four months there, along with Walter Benjamin's friend Alfred Cohn,[38] before his champion Charlotte Sempell managed to free him to return to Paris and Arendt in late December. In spite of a debilitating kidney infection, he proved his resilience in captivity, cheerfully writing to Arendt of sleeping under the stars and his happiness "when I think of the great reservoir of love" they had for each other.[39] When she chided him for scrimping on the details of his hardships in camp, he answered that at this "most dangerous period in the history of civilization," all special pleading had to give way to a more general viewpoint. "Let every man do his duty," he wrote.[40] "Above all, one shouldn't make too much of a fuss about oneself."[41]

Their reunion was short. The following May, after Germany invaded Belgium and launched its campaign against France, German residents were officially designated "enemy aliens" and moved by bus and train from holding pens in central Paris to prison camps on the Spanish border at Gurs, for women, and Le Vernet, for men. Martha was allowed to remain in Paris, because of age, but Arendt and Blücher, newly married, were separated with no means of communication between them or access to news of the world. Arendt contemplated suicide, she later wrote,[42] but summoning the pariah's virtues of stout heart and humor, she took to helping establish order in the grim, filthy, disease-ridden camp and so bolster courage against the twin lures of resignation and self-pity.

She spent four weeks at Gurs, where six thousand women

were interned. During the confusion of the French surrender in late June, chaos reigned; Arendt joined a group of women who laid hold of administrative exit papers and simply walked out of the camp. "None of us could 'describe' what lay in store for those who remained behind," she later wrote. "All that we could do was to tell them what we expected would happen — the camp would be handed over to the victorious Germans."[43] Only two hundred women left the camp as Arendt did; the rest chose to stay behind so that husbands and family could more easily find them. Vichy officials quickly took control, releasing some and permanently imprisoning others. That fall, Adolf Eichmann, the newly appointed SS officer in charge of the disposition of the Jews, transported almost seven thousand Jews from Baden, Germany — the entire Jewish population of the town — to Gurs, which subsequently became a German concentration camp. In 1942, most of those who survived were sent to extermination camps in the east, mainly Auschwitz.[44] Arendt had escaped Eichmann. Yet she was now stateless and without even a temporary home, one of "a new kind of human beings — the kind that are put in concentration camps by their foes and in internment camps by their friends."[45]

Blücher also escaped — peeling away from a forced march south from Le Vernet soon after the French surrender. The two reunited in the streets of Montauban, near Toulouse, where a Huguenot mayor bade welcome to political fugitives from all over France.[46] Old acquaintances turned up in town, including Anne Mendelssohn, now married to a professor and naturalized French citizen named Eric Weil, and Arendt's mother, who had managed to flee Paris under Nazi occupation. Like tens of thousands of other dispossessed German, Austrian, Czech, Belgian, Dutch, Polish, and French Jews, as well as political refugees like Blücher, they needed to get out of France and out of Europe to stay alive. The issue was made painfully clear to Arendt and Blücher when their brilliant friend Walter Benjamin took his life in a moment of despondency while trying unsuccessfully to cross out of Vichy France to Spain and freedom. Arendt wrote a poem in his memory, imagining listening in the darkness for soft "archaic melodies" of a sweeter time and place now passed.[47]

By then, it was nearly impossible for a traveler without papers to leave France. One of the best of the illegal routes was operated out of Marseilles by a thirty-two-year-old American literary journalist named Varian Fry. Beginning in June 1940, Fry, the Harvard-educated editor of a little poetry magazine called *Hound & Horn,* saw the coming crisis and took it on himself to raise funds, badger officials, hire forgers, bribe border guards, and supply credible French exit papers and American entry visas to more than a thousand trapped European scientists, artists, and activists, among them Marcel Duchamp, Arthur Koestler, Wanda Landowska, and Max Ophüls. Hannah, Heinrich, and Martha made several visits to Marseilles; with letters of reference supplied by Günther Stern in the United States, they finally won a spot on one of Fry's lists. Martha's U.S. entry visa was delayed, but Hannah and Heinrich, having both permission to leave France and enter America, immediately departed by train for the free port of Lisbon. In April 1941, they boarded a ship for New York City; Martha followed a few weeks later. In September, Fry's operation was shut down. By October, the borders of all the German-occupied nations of Europe, including France, were closed against Jewish "external" emigration. In December the first gas chambers were built at Chelmno. Fry, forced to return to New York, wrote one of the earliest and most electrifying accounts of American anti-immigration policy and the Nazi death machine. Called "The Massacre of the Jews," it was published in the *New Republic* in December 1942.

Fry also saved the lives of Édouard and Germaine de Rothschild and their daughter Bethsabée.[48] Perhaps Hannah was thinking of this when she wrote, in "We Refugees," "History has forced the status of outlaws upon both, upon pariahs and parvenus alike."[49] Martin Beerwald, who held fast to his home in Königsberg, died of a stroke in 1942, a few months before the remaining Jews of his city were transported by Eichmann to Auschwitz and near-certain death.[50]

5

Security and Fame

The Origins of Totalitarianism and the
New York Circle, 1941–1961

> Everything was possible and nothing was true.
> — HANNAH ARENDT, The Origins of Totalitarianism, 1951[1]

ANNAH ARENDT AND Heinrich Blücher arrived at the docks on New York City's bustling West Side in May 1941.[2] They had twenty-five dollars, clothing, photographs, and an unpublished collection of Walter Benjamin's essays, entrusted to Arendt by Benjamin before he left France for Spain. With a seventy-five-dollar monthly stipend guaranteed by a Zionist organization until they could find work, the pair rented two furnished rooms in a shabby redbrick rooming house on West Ninety-Fifth Street and waited for Martha, who arrived in June, thin, frightened, and exhausted.

For Arendt and her small family, the next three years were hard ones. Sharing two rooms and preparing meals in a communal kitchen, they lived meagerly and sought out friends of friends from Germany: Julie Vogelstein-Braun, the sister of a Königsberg rabbi who was relatively prosperous and knew her way around New York; Albert Salomon, a professor of sociology at the New School who had emigrated in 1935 and gave Blücher paid research assignments; the Columbia University historian Salo Baron, who encouraged Arendt to write for

German-language publications, even before she could communicate in English; Bertolt Brecht, who turned up in New York from time to time; and the political theorist Theodor Adorno. As she struggled to get her bearings, what impressed her most was that America, with its many varieties of immigrant peoples, was not a nation-state like the European nations — not unified by "blood and soil" and thousands of years of tribal history. It was a republic of citizens equally bound by a sworn allegiance to the U.S. Constitution, a document she, like many other new arrivals, revered.

Even before the war ended and the United States expanded its immigration quotas, she must have been surprised by the cosmopolitan character of New York City intellectual life. In the early and mid-1940s, the city was, as it had been at other times, "the beacon, the world city of freedom, openness, hope," according to Alfred Kazin. The Upper West Side, "the cheaper side of town" where Arendt lived, was, he added, "ethnic territory, foreign," and was filled with the sights and sounds of Europe.[3] In spite of hardships, the city welcomed Arendt.

She began to piece together a living, primarily by writing. The politics of antitotalitarianism became her subject. In a biweekly column for a Jewish German-language newspaper called *Aufbau,* she advocated for unified Jewish action in the battle against Hitler. Stateless, in a new country, with reason to worry that she or Blücher might be unfavorably noticed or even expelled, she took a public stance in favor of the unpopular movement to raise a Jewish army, comprising volunteers from all nations of the world to fight Hitler "as Jews, in Jewish battle formations under a Jewish flag."[4] *"[Y]ou can only defend yourself as the person you are attacked as,"* she wrote in *Aufbau,* pointing out that to expect a benefit from Hitler's defeat without making a contribution to it was "utopian," just as to anticipate a reward merely for suffering was apolitical and unworldly.[5] Reflecting hundreds of conversations with Blücher and friends like Blu-

menfeld and Benjamin in Paris, she regretted the long "pluto-
cratic regime" of the Jewish philanthropic class of Europe, such
as the Rothschilds, who for centuries had stood between the
Jewish people and the political realities of the nations in which
they lived.[6] A Jewish army would democratize Jewry and show
the world that "we too engage in politics."[7] Apolitical Jewish
"worldlessness" and a self-interested philanthropic class of Jewish "notables" became driving themes in Arendt's early political
writing and, eventually, in the most searing controversies of her
professional life.

   With Salo Baron's help, she also published essays on French
anti-Semitism and on minority rights in magazines with names
like *Jewish Social Studies* and *Contemporary Jewish Record*.[8] Together with *Aufbau,* she earned enough money to provide for
the household, supplemented by a weekly gift of sweets from Julie Vogelstein-Braun. ("First grub, then ethics," Heinrich would
later say, quoting the Marxist Brecht, and explaining: "First the
cake and then a theory for cutting it.")[9] Martha did most of the
cooking and cleaning and earned small sums from home-based
garment-industry piecework. She was slow to learn English and
so was Heinrich, who before finding employment as a research
aide to Salomon went off each day to shovel chemicals across
the river in a northern New Jersey factory. His research assignment, for a book on Axis military strategy, was at first demanding, then intermittent, then faded away. At home, he and Martha were at loggerheads. He was not pulling his weight. She was
bossy and "bourgeois." Much of the time, Hannah was the me-
diator and the primary, sometimes only, breadwinner.

   She mastered English quickly but not easily, and with
wrenching twists of syntax. Setting aside her native language
was a source of deepest grief. "When your Stradivarius has
been filched and you are forced to pay an incredible price for a
beer-fiddle," Blücher wrote to her soon after their arrival, "you
should at least refuse to start studying all over again just for a

license so you can play the beer-fiddle."[10] She studied, but she stood at an emotional distance from English all her life. To "put it extremely simply," she told Günter Gaus, "in German I know a rather large part of German poetry by heart; the poems are always somehow in the back of my mind. I can never do that again."[11] Yet the shocking experience of exile — of being "unwanted and unloved" by nations[12] — presented her with so many historical puzzles to ponder and so many new and pressing ideas to articulate that she eventually wrote eight major books and hundreds of essays in English. A classicist, an apostate philosopher, a reluctant academic, an ambivalent Zionist activist — in the end, above all, she became a great writer in a language not her own.

When she began to publish works in English — within a year of her arrival — the beautiful, bitter essays she wrote contained the product of the previous decade's compressed emotion, experience, discussion, and self-directed reading of European history and thought, from Hobbes and Kant to Varnhagen, Clausewitz, and Marx. The essays were printed — with considerable grammatical help from editors — in *Partisan Review, Menorah Journal, Commentary,* and the *Nation.* Her little-read essay "We Refugees," describing the polite desperation of hunted, stateless persons in a world of states, is among the finest things she ever wrote. An early article for *Partisan Review,* called "What Is Existenz Philosophy," is among her densest.[13] It was assigned as an introduction to the work of Jean-Paul Sartre, who had published *Being and Nothingness* in France in 1943 and whose charming story "The Root of the Chestnut Tree" preceded her essay in the same issue. Instead, she wrote a brief history of German existentialism, emphasizing the work of Martin Heidegger and Karl Jaspers, both unknown to Americans, with Heidegger cast in the role of an ego-besotted malevolent genius and Jaspers as an enlightened humanist. In light of the rise of the Nazis, she wrote that Heidegger's neo-Romantic infatuation with an "authentic self" in opposition to the ordinary social life of his time was a betrayal of the human; and it was only a step from intellectual annihilation of the human to a nihilism that made possible physical annihilation by Hitler.[14] Such was her anger at the time. Philip Rahv, the coeditor of *Partisan Review,* objected to the essay and to its Germanic title; Arendt stood her ground, and Rahv, a Ukrainian former Communist literary brawler, backed down. "She was a redoubtable woman," recalled William Barrett.[15]

One thing she wasn't: a careerist. She made little attempt to please. Yet instead of freezing her out, Rahv and his circle invited her to editorial luncheons, left-wing organizing committee meetings, and cocktail parties, where she dazzled the tight-knit group of largely Jewish New York intellectuals, most notably the men, with her brains. The poet Delmore Schwartz called her a "Weimar Republic flapper" and tried to stay out of her way,[16] but for Alfred Kazin, Irving Howe, Lionel Trilling, Paul Goodman, Randall Jarrell, and even Saul Bellow, who came to detest her after the Eichmann book, she was a bold and cultivated witness to the European catastrophe, the unimaginable horrors of which were becoming clearer to Americans by the month, and an avatar of the European philosophical tradition. She read Aristotle in Greek and Hegel in German. She was as "womanly as she was acute," wrote Kazin.[17] The New York intellectuals took her in and idolized her, at least until disagreements over the founding of Israel in 1948 led to a temporary chill. There was little question of her commitment to the Jewish cause in the eyes of those New Yorkers of the mid-1940s, especially after she took a full-time job as the research director and later the executive director of the Commission on European Jewish Cultural Reconstruction, a branch of Salo Baron's Conference on Jewish Relations,[18] where her mission was to compile a list of European Jewish cultural treasures that had been stolen and that might yet be rescued from the devastation at war's end. "She was a blazing Jew," according to Alfred Kazin.[19]

More than a few acquaintances, particularly women, remembered her in a cooler light. Diana Trilling felt upstaged and excluded by her.[20] Kazin's third wife, Ann Birstein, thought her "an ugly, bossy German refugee" with "ears [that] popped out of her hairdo" and a proud contempt for American culture.[21] Even William Barrett, who was fond of her, admitted that she "had her prejudices." He observed that "she was a German Jew, with the peculiar double loyalty" that membership in that selective group characteristically produced. In the tradition of Friedrich Nietzsche, she revered German Jews as "'Good Europeans,' the dedicated bearers of the intellectual culture of the West."[22]

She was certainly ablaze when she met her future best friend Mary McCarthy at a party given by Philip Rahv in the spring of 1945.[23] McCarthy, thirty-two years old, quick-witted, chic, a magnet for men although temporarily married to Edmund Wilson, was *Partisan Review*'s drama critic and a grand dame of left-wing causes. In her first book of stories, *The Company She Keeps,* the central story, "The Man in the Brooks Brothers Shirt," scandalized readers with its scene of a naked young woman waking hung over beside a boorish middle-aged traveling salesman in a railway car. As Arendt stood amid a clutch of guests, the former Vassar girl casually joked about Hitler's apparent desire to be loved by his enemies, especially the French. McCarthy, with enemies of her own, was making the point that it was foolish to expect goodwill for bad. "Poor Hitler," she said, at which Arendt, perhaps not used to stylish sarcasm, erupted. "How can you say such a thing to me, a victim of Hitler, a person who has been in a concentration camp?"—for by that time she would have known that Gurs had come under Nazi control. To Rahv, her host (and, as most knew, McCarthy's former lover), she said, "How can you have this kind of conversation in your home,

you, a Jew?" McCarthy "slunk away," she later recalled.²⁴ The
two women didn't speak again for four years. Then one evening, while they were waiting for a subway train after a strategy
session for Dwight Macdonald's magazine *politics,* they struck
up a conversation and discovered they liked each other. They
would remain deeply loyal confidantes for thirty years. During
and in the aftermath of the Eichmann trial, it was to McCarthy,
sometimes even in preference to Blücher, whom Arendt turned
to test her theories and pour out her shock, anger, confusion,
and contempt.

    "Blazing" as Arendt might have been, however, Kazin and
the *Partisan Review* editors missed some early signs of unconventional thinking beyond the call for a Jewish army. Beginning in 1944, she published a group of essays in which she first
sought the origins of totalitarianism, including an essay on modern "Race-Thinking"²⁵ and another called "Concerning Minorities."²⁶ These essays rejected the standard notion that the Nazis exemplified an especially vicious modern form of universal
anti-Semitism — in fact, the essays scarcely mentioned the Nazis or the Jews. The problem was broader, as she saw it, and at
its heart was the modern European nation-state, which from its
beginnings had excluded from full citizenship all but a specific
kind of human being — German, French, Slav. By extension, it
had created marginalized minority populations in every nation,
thousands of men and women who did not "belong." Minorities without rights — native-born illegal aliens — could be protected by laws; but without a founding constitution, those laws
could be changed. At times such minorities could be economically useful to the ruling class, but they could also be blamed
when things went wrong and selectively stripped of civil and
economic liberties. The problem deepened after World War I,
when the victorious allies divided European empires into new,
small, sometimes arbitrarily delineated states with "no right
of residence or consular protection of any sort" for groups of

people who had lived on the land for generations.[27] Thus, by implication, in Arendt's view, the Jews of Europe were exemplary rather than an exceptional minority, at least with respect to statelessness and vulnerability.

But why, then, she asked, did Hitler train his fury on the Jews? In a 1946 essay called "Privileged Jews,"[28] she proposed a partial answer, one that was erudite, powerful, and yet so deeply against the grain that the essay was renamed "The Moral of History" when it was republished in Arendt's *The Jewish Writings* in 2007. From the Age of Enlightenment through the nineteenth century, she wrote, before and during the time of Rahel Varnhagen, "court" Jews had earned special privileges in exchange for special favors to the state, primarily financial favors. Such "exception Jews," as she also called them, whose wealth — until Hitler — allowed them to purchase immunity from "the common destiny of the Jewish people,"[29] aided disaster in two ways. First, their material possessions and deep if narrow political influence stirred the envy of non-Jewish citizens. Second, because they also became Jewish civic leaders and philanthropists who mediated with the state on behalf of all the Jews, they placed themselves as a wall between their poorer fellows and political experience with the state, including the experience of petitioning for rights. As the fortunes of bankers such as the Rothschilds grew, Arendt wrote, they "had greater need for the poverty of the Jewish masses as a protective argument. The poorer the masses became, the more secure the rich Jews felt and the brighter their glory shone."[30] Of course, in the end the "privileged Jews" were not exempt from the Nazi scourge, but they had helped to make the Jewish people as a whole Hitler's failsafe choice of a political scapegoat.

If these ideas seem familiar now, it is only because Arendt made them so when she published *The Origins of Totalitarianism* in 1951. In the mid-1940s, few if any of her American friends registered a reaction to them, perhaps because at the time her argument seemed more Marxist than anti-Jewish or because the history of European Jewry was unfamiliar to the American children and grandchildren of immigrants; but after Eichmann it struck a nerve. As for the assimilated Jews of Max Arendt's generation, "they maintained they were able to be 'men like others on the street but Jews at home.'"[31] To Hannah Arendt, it was now clear that they had been mistaken — in Europe, at least, if not in the United States. So were the European "Jews of education," both during Varnhagen's time and during her own, some of whom had felt themselves exempted from "Jewishness" by virtue of having become exceptional in their mastery of the German and Western canon. Although she was proud of her Königsberg heritage and of her own extraordinary generation of Jewish intellectuals' "almost complete assimilation" into German high culture, and even "harbored nostalgia for that condition and that period," according to William Barrett,[32] she was convinced that European Jews "always had to pay for social glory with political misery and for political success with social insult."[33] With the rise of Hitler, the Gestapo's boot advanced to halt the seesaw. For the Jews of Europe, assimilation had been an illusion.

In a second series of essays, collected in *The Jewish Writings,* Arendt celebrated the virtues of the pariah in a world of strivers. In some of these essays, she traced the ahistorical — indeed, mythic — character of the "conscious pariah" as a spiritual truth teller to the dreamers of assimilation and the defenders of privilege and passivity, especially in the work of poets and authors such as Heinrich Heine and Franz Kafka. These essays were personal and heartfelt. Their thesis was simple. The Third Reich had proved that every Jew was an outcast. "The pariah Jew and the parvenu Jew are in the same boat, rowing desperately in the same angry sea," she wrote. "Both are branded with the same mark; both alike are outlaws."[34] Far better to be a *conscious* pariah in the tradition of Heine, Kafka, the theorist Ber-

nard Lazare, and her "best friend" Rahel Varnhagen than to
cling reflexively to outworn hope or illusion. "All vaunted Jewish qualities — the 'Jewish heart,' humanity, humor, disinterested intelligence — are pariah qualities," she wrote. "All Jewish
shortcomings — tactlessness, political stupidity, inferiority complexes, and money-grubbing — are characteristics of upstarts."[35]
Collectively, the way to transform misfortune into strength was
to turn unchosen ostracism into collective rebellion — as with a
Jewish army.[36] She could be a harsh critic of any apparent political apathy or "worldlessness" among the Jewish population of
Europe and America or, by extension, any group of people who
expected to have their rights bestowed and/or safeguarded by
someone other than themselves. "From the 'disgrace' of being a
Jew there is but one escape — to fight for the honor of the Jewish
people as a whole," she wrote in January 1943, in an essay on Stefan Zweig, a refugee who, like Benjamin, committed suicide.[37]

By then, she and Blücher knew about the network of
German-operated concentration camps and the forced expulsion of Jews from Germany and conquered territories to camps
in Poland and the east. They had heard of Adolf Eichmann. In
1943, they began to hear about the death camps. "At first we
didn't believe it," she told Gaus, not only because it was monstrous but also "because militarily it was unnecessary and un-
called for. My husband . . . said don't be gullible. . . . They can't
go that far!" Six months later, with the Russian advance into Poland, "we had the proof," she said. "It was really as if an abyss
had opened." The discovery of mechanized factories explicitly for killing — for "the fabrication of corpses," as she put it —
without any practical political or military purpose became a
turning point for her. "You know, what was decisive was not the
year 1933, at least not for me," she said. "What was decisive was
the day we learned about Auschwitz."[38]

In response, she gathered many of her essays on the history
of the Jews as a minority people in Europe, outlined additional

material, and toward the end of 1944 sent a proposal to Houghton Mifflin for a book she called "The Elements of Shame: Anti-Semitism — Imperialism — Racism," or "The Three Pillars of Hell," or simply "A History of Totalitarianism." At the suggestion of a Houghton Mifflin editor, the book became *The Origins of Totalitarianism,* a title that never fully pleased her; she thought it suggested a kind of historical predictability or inevitability that she did not believe in. The extermination camps were anything but predictable, except in retrospect. It was the book that made her famous.

The war in Europe ended in May 1945, and Arendt's work at the Commission on European Jewish Cultural Reconstruction intensified. From an office in the rundown Manhattan neighborhood around Columbus Circle, surrounded by cigar stores and junk shops,[39] Arendt interviewed refugees and scholars who had knowledge of pre-Reich synagogues, archives, and museums and recorded their recollections, from which she and her colleagues eventually published a two-hundred-page "Tentative List of Jewish Cultural Treasures in Axis-Occupied Countries"[40] to guide postwar investigators in recovery efforts. She used the insights she gained about German methods of covering up official thievery, including bureaucratic sleights of hand devised by Eichmann, to describe the "planned shapelessness" and layered impenetrability of totalitarian regimes in *Origins.*[41] At the same time, she was reading personal accounts by camp survivors[42] and grappling with the camps' uncanny power to destroy the human personality — indeed, to reduce individual human beings to mere "bundles of reactions [that] can be exchanged at random for any other" — in people who had been displaced, stripped bare, starved, and tormented without reference to personal innocence or guilt and without hope of redress.[43] One of the great insights of *Origins* was that the camps "are the laboratories where changes in human nature are tested" and "total domination" of the human spirit is proved to be attainable.[44]

She called the experiment with total domination "radical evil," her most famous phrase until she coined "the banality of evil" to characterize the apparent triviality of Eichmann's inner life when measured against his crimes.

There had been other factors at work in this historical catastrophe. Arendt argued that the era's political dislocations and widespread unemployment had made millions of Germans both "economically superfluous and socially burdensome,"[45] and helped to make it possible for the Nazi Party to strip both Jews and Gentiles of their dignity, sense of meaning, and, finally, lives. Twenty years after that, in *Eichmann,* she argued that if the Nazi lieutenant colonel in charge of transporting Jews had not found his own life to be as meaningless as those whose lives he abetted in taking, he could not have become the "desk murderer" she had seen on trial in Jerusalem.

She had always worked hard. In the postwar years, from 1945 until the early 1950s, she worked at an almost superhuman pace. While compiling lists and writing *Origins,* she became a senior editor in the newly established New York office of Schocken Books, where she edited the diaries of Franz Kafka and the scholarly work of Gershom Scholem, among other projects, and tried intermittently to talk the firm's cautious founder and her friend, Salman Schocken, into translating into English and publishing Benjamin's manuscript of essays (something the firm declined to do until after Schocken's death in 1959). She became an ad hoc academic after all, teaching European history part-time to graduate students at Brooklyn College. She joined Judah Magnes's Unity movement for a binational Israel as its political adviser,[46] which entailed writing papers and drafting speeches advocating a negotiated settlement between Palestinian Jews and Arabs. She crafted another, related series of essays, not incorporated into *Origins,* arguing against the creation of an exclusively Jewish state in Palestine. "A home that my neighbor does not recognize and respect is not a home," the still-stateless Arendt wrote.[47] "The independence of Palestine can be achieved only on a solid basis of Jewish-Arab cooperation."[48] She chided the traditionally quarrelsome Zionists for their false show of consensus in this matter, as they feared the political use their enemies might make of open discord. "[M]ass unanimity is not the result of agreement," she wrote, "but an expression of fanaticism and hysteria."[49]

This time, her American friends noticed her rebellion. Her stance and tone of voice brought her a first, tart taste of their disapproval. Greenberg, an editor at *Commentary* (and later a famous art critic), rejected one of her essays, preposterously citing "anti-Semitic implications,"[50] and delayed publishing another.[51] *Aufbau* canceled her column. The previously friendly left-wing journal *Jewish Frontier* denounced her. She attracted the public anger of the Zionist historian and jurist Jacob Robinson, who later denounced *Eichmann in Jerusalem*.[52] The controversy faded after Israel was established by UN partition, although she later told Ann Birstein that she was briefly on an Irgun hit list.[53]

In the years that followed, Arendt's "little tribe" of friends grew larger and more devoted. But in May 1948, the month of Israel's founding, in a biographical note in *Commentary,* she publicly identified herself as a Zionist for the last time.[54] Henceforth, when "attacked as a Jew," she would identify and defend herself as a Jew but would otherwise regard her Jewishness as she characterized it to Gershom Scholem: "one of the indisputable factual data" of her life that did not matter to her "in the least" on a personal and individual level.[55]

Arendt's mother observed her increasing bluntness of speech and manner with alarm and blamed Arendt's overwork and Blücher's working-class manners for the change. This wasn't fully accurate: The shy, eager, though determined younger Arendt had learned through harsh experience to face circumstances squarely and speak plainly from the least obstructed vantage point she could attain. The more active she was, how-

ever, the more her mother and Blücher were thrown together in
the rooms on West Ninety-Fifth Street. Martha had made few
friends and was isolated and critical. Blücher, without work and
given to fits of "melancholy" in the postwar years, did nothing
but "read and read"[56] and often seemed effectively paralyzed, as
Arendt noted in a sympathetic letter to him in 1946.[57] (His melancholy had "erupted immediately over the gas chambers," she
wrote to Kurt Blumenfeld in Jerusalem. She added, "It is sel-
dom that people are able to help each other, mutually; but in
our case, I think it is really true that both of us would, without
the other, scarcely have survived.")[58] She might well have been
thinking of Blücher when she observed about Leo Jogiches during a fallow period in *his* life that he "felt impotent and superfluous when there was nothing to do." Rosa Luxemburg would
have been the last to hold this against her lover, Arendt wrote.
"The members of [the Spartacist League] did not judge one another in these categories."[59] Neither did she. Martha, however —
former Spartacan that she was — did judge. Seeing too little of
her daughter and too much of Blücher and able to travel outside
the United States for the first time since the war, she booked
passage on a ship bound for England in the summer of 1948.
Her intention was to live with her stepdaughter Eva Beerwald,
who had found refuge in London in 1938.

Martha suffered from asthma. She had an acute attack on-
board ship and died a few days after arriving in London. In late
July 1948, Eva Beerwald sent a telegram reading, "Mother died
sleeping last night — arranging cremation."[60] She was seventy-
four years old. She had once been musical, adventurous, and liberal in spirit. She had grown plaintive in confinement to a culture that was foreign and seemed brash. She was one of "we
refugees" about whom Hannah had written in 1943: "We lost
our home, which means the familiarity of daily life. We lost our
occupation, which means the confidence that we are of some use
in this world. We lost our language, which means . . . the simplic-

ity of gestures. . . ." With Martha's death, Hannah also lost her last connection to a timeless period of her childhood, before disease, war, displacement, and flight arose from "this mad world" that she was determined both to understand and to explain.[61]

Even her native city vanished from the map: Soviet Russia had impounded a battered Königsberg at Potsdam for use as a naval outpost, renamed it Kaliningrad, and sealed it off against visitors. She was still stateless, having yet to be naturalized in America. Her home then, and for the rest of their lives, was with Blücher. "Snubby—for God's sake, you are my four walls," she wrote to him the following year.[62] He answered, "I need the four walls with you more, much more, than you do."[63] Practically speaking, this was true.

Blücher gradually recovered his energy and panache. Arendt was secluded at Dartmouth College in Hanover, New Hampshire, working on *Origins* when Martha died. He wrote to her in a confessional mode. "I started having a bad conscience," he admitted. "The old woman . . . pointed out to me, a little too clearly, the limited but powerful justification of the bourgeois standpoint. . . . But what really infuriated me was the way she always sucked your blood, and her total lack of respect for your incredible accomplishments."[64] Within days of Martha's death he experienced a "crazed attack, or better still, an assault of productivity" that eventually landed him a stable teaching job in art history and philosophy at the experimental New School for Social Research in New York and thereafter led to a long and satisfying association with Bard College, a hive of intellectual energy a hundred miles north of New York City on the Hudson River. By all accounts, he was a great and inspiring teacher.[65] He remained insecure, however, and with good reason.[66] With no diploma, a heavily doctored résumé, and a complicated German Communist past, he rightly viewed himself as a moving target for postwar anticommunists in both the United States and Europe. Late in the summer of Arendt's mother's death, he had an affair with a younger Russian Jewish woman, one of a number of love affairs he conducted during his marriage to Arendt but possibly the first one she discovered, apparently through common friends; she was crushed and angry but proved resilient about this, too.

She completed *The Origins of Totalitarianism* in the fall of 1949.[67] In some ways the book, Arendt's majestic effort to penetrate beneath the horrors of her age, is a meditation on loneliness, on metaphysical rootlessness, on not belonging — a theme that resonates at least as powerfully now as it did then. In it, she tries to understand what she admits defies understanding: the demonic wish to make men superfluous to others and themselves. Each of its three sections is a study in the growing dispensability of groups of Europeans from the eighteenth century forward. In the first part, "Antisemitism," she traces the changing uses of Jews — those ancient scapegoats — from religious to political outcasts, with the result that by the late 1800s they came to represent and also to foreshadow modern homelessness in all its emanations; here she incorporates her earlier insights into privileged Jews, pariahs, and parvenus to demonstrate the ways in which narrowly defined self-interest can blind vulnerable people to fateful political changes. In "Imperialism," she depicts the power of nineteenth- and twentieth-century industrial development to displace traditional aristocracies and create a featureless, rootless bourgeoisie, which itself became politically and economically expendable. In "Totalitarianism," the third and last section, she writes — soaringly and with biblical inflection — "It bases itself on loneliness, on the experience of not belonging to the world at all, which is among the most radical and desperate experiences of man." Chronic unemployment, inflation and punitive taxation, the debasement or suppression of a public forum for action and debate, the dislocation that comes from moving from nation to nation or job to job, the imposed inconsequence of innocence and guilt, in groups and out groups, the threat of terror—all tools of totalitarian dominance—seem to prepare victims and bullies alike to undervalue their lives.

But it was the death camps that altered everything. They were the dark laboratories "where changes in human nature are tested," she wrote.

> When the impossible was made possible [by the camps] it became the unpunishable, the unforgivable absolute evil which could no longer be understood and explained by the [ordinary] evil motives of self-interest, greed, covetousness, resentment, lust for power, and cowardice; and which therefore anger could not revenge, love could not endure, friendship could not forgive. Just as the victims in the death factories or the holes of oblivion are no longer "human" in the eyes of their executioners, so this newest species of criminals is beyond the pale even of solidarity in human sinfulness.[68]

Elsewhere in the book she wrote, "Everything was possible and nothing was true."[69]

She dedicated the book to her husband, who—having "read and read" throughout the 1940s—had contributed much to its command of twentieth-century political and military history, the failures of state socialism, and the rise of a peculiarly "selfless" mass man who was susceptible to totalitarian manipulation.[70]

Published in the spring of 1951, *The Origins of Totalitarianism* also deconstructed Soviet totalitarianism, although some viewed the passages on Stalinist terror as an afterthought. It was widely and ecstatically praised. In *Commentary*, David Riesman, whose 1950 book *The Lonely Crowd* first classified "inner-" and "outer-directed" personalities and influenced a generation of thinkers, placed her in the company of theorists such as Freud, Nietzsche, and Comte.[71] Dwight Macdonald declared that her insights signaled the greatest advance in social thinking since

Karl Marx. Susan Sontag's future husband, Philip Rieff, described the book as "a vast spiritualization of history" comparable to Oswald Spengler's *The Decline of the West*.[72] A famous review by the antipositivist Eric Voegelin, whose influence Arendt had earlier acknowledged in her essay on "Race-Thinking" in 1944, described the section on anti-Semitism as the best short history of the problem in existence. And in *The Origins of Totalitarianism*, wrote Voegelin, she had provided a piercing depiction of the spiritual dissolution of the human personality, "from the early anti-bourgeois and anti-Semitic resentment to the contemporary horrors of the 'man who does his duty' and of his victims."[73] It remains the most passionate, complex, moving, and influential account ever written of the clash between civilization and official barbarism in twentieth-century Europe.

In intellectual circles, the book made Arendt an icon almost overnight. Requests to teach and lecture poured in from Princeton and the University of Chicago, Berkeley, Harvard, and the New School. In spite of her earlier wish to steer clear of philosophers and academicians, she wore gracefully the role of the public intellectual and ever after earned her livelihood by teaching. The years of returning home at night to furnished rooms gave way to a more comfortable existence; first, she and Blücher rented a small apartment on Morningside Drive, sunless and overlooking a piano factory but complete with a kitchen and furnished by themselves, with a portrait of Kafka in the entry hall.[74] Then, in 1959, they moved into five large, sunny rooms on Riverside Drive, each with a view of the Hudson River. Arendt became a U.S. citizen in December 1951, Blücher in August 1952.

The book completed at last, Arendt took her first trip back to Europe since arriving in New York, flying to Paris on a mission to conduct field research for the agency for Jewish Cultural Reconstruction. She found Paris surprisingly unaltered, if in deeper disrepair: shabby, expensive, ill-tempered, a city without heat or hot water, but stunningly beautiful. ("When I walked into the small, shabby Place des Ternes, I almost cried at seeing a *Place* again," she wrote to Blücher.)[75] By late November, she was in Germany. Based in the American zone at Wiesbaden and adhering to a grueling travel schedule of one- and two-day suitcase stops to inspect libraries and museums in Bonn, Frankfurt, Nuremberg, Würzburg, Heidelberg, and Berlin, "with appointments from morning to night," she felt less at home than lost and disoriented, she wrote to Blücher.[76] On the one hand, she experienced "indescribable joy" at hearing German spoken in the streets.[77] A "lump of sentimentality" rose in her throat at dear, familiar sights ("one's feet know so well which way to go"), but she was distressed by the almost universal "gloating" she observed, even in the midst of the bombed-out, pulverized remains of a thousand years of German history.[78] Suddenly, every man, woman, and child had become a lifelong pacifist and was surviving on "illusions and stupidity"—the latter signifying what she considered to be a characteristic lack of authentic feeling on the part of postwar Germans, especially an absence of empathy.[79] When confronted with a Jew (there were only thirty-seven thousand left in Germany in 1950),[80] the average man on the street, she discovered, let loose "a deluge of stories about how Germans have suffered" and drew up a balance sheet "between German suffering and the suffering of others, the implication being that one side cancels the other." She was repelled. The aftermath of totalitarian rule in Germany was a terrible shared conviction that "all facts can be changed and all lies can be made true" and a cynical assumption that every opinion about events under Hitler was as good or as bad as every other. This indifference to truth was "the most striking and frightening aspect of the German flight from reality," she wrote in an essay for *Commentary*.[81] After the first two weeks she was ready to go home to Blücher.[82]

She didn't go. Instead, just before Christmas she crossed into Switzerland to reunite with her dear old professor Karl Jaspers, now teaching at the University of Basel. Jaspers, by birth a north German Protestant, was the antithesis of the "suffering Germans" Arendt met: An anti-Nazi and the devoted husband of a Jew, he had ended his friendship with Martin Heidegger on principle in 1936, had been forbidden by the Nazis from teaching in German universities in 1937, and had voluntarily renounced his German citizenship after the war, in 1948. No one in Europe was reading Jaspers's work, she wrote to Blücher, begging him to send a note of appreciation to the aging philosopher about his latest book. On the other hand, Germany was "flooded again" with Heidegger.[83]

Back in Germany, Arendt met Heidegger for the first time in twenty years. He was sixty; she was forty-four. She was visiting Freiburg for two days and wavered about whether to get in touch with him: The stories Jaspers had told her, including one about his cool treatment of Jaspers's wife during the 1930s, infuriated her. On impulse, she sent a note by hand, and a few hours later Heidegger appeared at her hotel. They drove to his house, from which his wife, Elfride, was absent. They conversed late into the night and pledged their love to each other.[84] The reunion was "the confirmation of an entire life," she wrote to him a few days later.[85] She returned to her hotel that night, "half asleep," and the next day took a hired car back to his house to see Elfride, at the philosopher's beseeching. The women argued: It's not clear what was said, but it was "personal,"[86] it was hostile, and at one point Elfride bizarrely suggested that they summon the estranged Karl Jaspers from Switzerland to act as referee, as Arendt afterward recalled in a letter to her former lover.[87] Arendt showed restraint, merely pointing out that Elfride had never made a secret of her anti-Semitism; but when writing to Blücher she blamed the "absolutely horrendous" woman both for making Heidegger's life "a hell on

earth" and, for the first time, for his record of Nazi collabora-
tion.[88] "Headline: Alliance between mob and elite," she wrote
to her husband, invoking the title of a chapter in *Origins* called
"The Temporary Alliance between the Mob and the Elite" to
convey her judgment that Heidegger was one of a "terrifying
roster of distinguished men" whom totalitarianism had won
over.[89] In her view, he was really the captive of a primitive, *volk-
ish,* unthinking mob of one, Elfride, who, if she had no other
virtues, at least had the grace not to belong to the despised category of middle-class "mass man." Thus began the rehabilitation
of Martin Heidegger in Arendt's mind and, to the degree she
was able to exert influence upon public opinion, in the respectable world.

She saw him again a month later and at intervals for the remainder of their lives. On each visit, he heaped on her unpublished manuscripts, untranslated articles and books, his griev-
ances against the world, and sometimes effusive thanks; she
acted as his unofficial agent and public advocate, especially in
the United States, where she helped to create his reputation and
championed the publication of his books. She was deferential,
if impatient. In later years, she often waited for a signal before
visiting or writing to him, as if still waiting for the light to ap-
pear in his study; she let the rhythms of his work and moods set
the pace and intensity of their encounters and correspondence.
Whatever he said to her during their first discussion of his Nazi
years — probably a version of his testimony before a denazifi-
cation committee in 1945, that is, that he had joined the Nazi
Party to enhance its appreciation of philosophy and to protect
the University of Freiburg, and had resigned as rector when
Nazi materialism and race hatred began to predominate[90] — it
is likely that she believed him no more or less than the committee did. The French-appointed committee revoked his license
to lecture from 1945 to 1949 and reinstated it with the designa-
tion "Fellow traveler. No punitive measures."[91] Her verdict was

more damning, in its way. To Jaspers, she wrote, "What you call [Heidegger's impure soul] I would call lack of character—but in the sense that he literally has none and certainly not a particularly bad one. At the same time, he lives in depths and with a passionateness that one can't easily forget."[92]

In a 1950s diary entry, written as a parable entitled "Heidegger the Fox," Arendt wickedly sketched a human animal "so lacking in slyness that he not only kept getting caught in traps but couldn't even tell the difference between a trap and a non-trap" and so devoid of normal fox fur (read: thin-skinned) that "he was completely without natural protection against the hardships of a fox's life." His ingenious solution: "He built a trap as his burrow"—presumably a reference not only to Heidegger's party membership but also to his home life with Elfride.[93] In letters from New York during her first few visits, Blücher encouraged her to befriend her former lover and to believe that he needed her friendship as a counterbalance to his folly and his wife—perhaps for reasons of Blücher's own. Heidegger led her to believe the same.

The nature of their private reconciliation is hinted in their letters. In "The Shadows," she had told him that she "did not belong to anything, anywhere, ever."[94] During their first evening together in Freiburg, she had said she felt not like a German ("I have never considered myself a German woman") or a Jew ("I have long since stopped") but "like who I really am, a girl from faraway"—the title of a poem by Friedrich Schiller.[95]

Heidegger replied with a poem of his own with the same name.

> *The stranger,*
> *Even to yourself,*
> *She is:*
> *Mountain of joy, sea of sorrow,*
> *Desert of desire,*

Dawn of arrival.
Stranger: home of the one gaze
Where the world begins.[96]

Some years later, in a striking passage in her second book, *The Human Condition* (1958), she meditated on forgiveness, perhaps with Heidegger in mind. "Without being forgiven," she reflected, or "released from the consequences of what we have done," the human capacity to act would be "confined to one single deed from which we could never recover; we would remain the victims of its consequences forever, not unlike the sorcerer's apprentice who lacked the magic formula to break the spell."[97] Arendt forgave Heidegger; in doing so, she set her world at rights again.[98] The "hidden king" was never far from her mind when she contemplated the importance of thinking, acting, and judging, the pivotal themes of her later years. She did not forget his lack of character, particularly on those occasions when he greeted her growing fame in Europe with a burst of petulance or periods of stony silence. "I know that it is intolerable for him that my name appears in public, that I write books, etc.," she wrote to Jaspers in 1961.[99] But her "road was wide and ran through the world," and it easily encompassed him.

She visited Europe often, spending vacations with Jaspers in Switzerland, with Anne Mendelssohn in France, and with Edna Brocke's mother, Käthe Fuerst, in Greece and Israel, giving lectures and accepting honors from eagerly, even unctuously, repentant Germans, culminating in the prestigious Lessing Prize from the city of Hamburg in 1959. She might have been speaking of herself when, in accepting the prize, she said of the Enlightenment poet and playwright Gotthold Lessing that he "never felt at home in the world as it then existed and probably never wanted to, and still after his own fashion he always remained committed to it."[100]

In New York, she entertained a parade of old and new

friends, including Hans Jonas, Robert Lowell, and Arthur Schlesinger Jr., with her patented brand of hospitality, urging on all comers "assorted nuts, chocolates, candied ginger, tea, coffee, Campari, whiskey, cigarettes, cake, crackers, fruit, cheese, almost all at once, regardless of conventional sequence or, often, of the time of day," recalled Mary McCarthy,[101] who was a frequent houseguest and a constant correspondent and loved to gossip with her high-minded friend about American politics, mutual acquaintances, men, and the meaning of Truth. Arendt wrote and published *The Human Condition,* in which she elegantly reclaimed a Greek perspective on human dignity, honor, and freedom in the public sphere as a brace against the dreariness of modern politics and social welfare, and revised and translated into English *Rahel Varnhagen: The Life of a Jewess.* In 1961, she published *Between Past and Future: Six Exercises in Political Thought,* on subjects then widely debated and now regarded as impossibly lofty—"What Is Authority?" "What Is Freedom?" "The Crisis in Culture," and "Tradition and the Modern Age"—before deciding to turn her hand to journalism and to report on the Eichmann trial.

These were largely years of peace and prosperity for Arendt. She taught self-structured courses on Plato and Aristotle, Kant, Spinoza, Hobbes, Machiavelli, revolution, and phenomenology at prestigious institutions across the country. She was an old-fashioned teacher who, like Heidegger, could turn a rigid hour-long lecture format into a brilliant display of ideas by the originality of her insights and the force of her personality,[102] although her theme remained constant: how the decisive break with the great Western tradition of honor, faith, and justice had permitted the elements of totalitarian to rise.

Arendt and Blücher spent summers on Cape Cod with McCarthy or in the little town of Palenville in the Catskill Mountains, which reminded visitors of a quaint German village. Otherwise, the couple was often apart. Blücher was wildly popular at Bard, earning commendations as a teacher and raises every year from 1952 until he taught his last class in 1969. He continued to have affairs throughout the 1950s and possibly the early 1960s, but it didn't occur to Arendt to divorce him, "a practice she found absurdly American," according to her literary executor, Lotte Kohler.[103] She resisted the entreaties of the squadrons of anticommunists and neoconservatives of the day to join their various causes and denounced them, risking drawing unwanted attention to herself and Blücher at a period when congressional committees and the Justice Department were still actively investigating naturalized citizens for alien sympathies. At the height of the McCarthy period, she specifically targeted ex-Communists — and tacitly defended her husband — in a review of *Witness,* Whittaker Chambers's titanic spiritual autobiography and confession of his years as an underground Communist spy. Arendt disapproved of the rehabilitated Chambers's role as an informant against Alger Hiss, and she wrote that the old Communist Party hardliners and the new ex-Communists had certain unsavory traits in common, including a totalitarian-tempered drive to change the world by force of will, "that is, to *make* mankind's future," and a reliance on police state tactics. In contrast, "former" Communists — like Blücher, although she didn't say so — "neither looked for a substitute for a lost faith" nor tried to persuade their dearest friends to join them in a new, oppositional, apocalyptic cause. "It is against these *makers of history* that a free society has to defend itself," she wrote, for men and women with a totalitarian drive to certainty will always insist that in order to "fight the dragon" one must "become a dragon" and will always be tempted to strangle the life out of "America, this republic," and the freedom to "live and let live," which it promises to the nabob and the pariah alike.[104]

6

After Eichmann
New York, 1963–1975

What do I fear? Myself? There's none else by.
Richard loves Richard: that is, I am I.
Is there a murderer here? No. Yes, I am:
Then fly. What from myself? Great reason why—
Lest I revenge. What, myself upon myself?
O no! Alas, I rather hate myself
For hateful deeds committed by myself.
I am a villain. Yet I lie, I am not.
Fool, of thyself speak well. Fool, do not flatter.

— RICHARD III, quoted by Hannah Arendt,
"Thinking and Moral Considerations," 1971[1]

HANNAH ARENDT'S HEART, humor, intelligence, and stamina carried her through the period immediately following the Eichmann trial and publication of *Eichmann in Jerusalem.* She took up the threads of her public life, a little more wary of fame, a little more protective of her closest private friendships, and with a strengthened determination to express the essence of a lifetime of thinking about human dignity, rebellion, unconventionality, and freedom.

In the fall of 1963, she began a five-year teaching assignment for the Committee on Social Thought at the University of Chicago. She lived and ate her meals in the Quadrangle Club on the great neo-Gothic campus, where Paul Tillich or Hans Morgenthau would sometimes join her for dinner. But otherwise she ate alone. Her peers on the committee — her friend the art critic Harold Rosenberg, to whose criticism of *Eichmann* she listened one long afternoon without saying a word but with "her hands like claws," he later told a common acquaintance,[2] and Saul Bellow, who had never warmed to her but who shared her passion for politics — were distant for a time but, along with other professors such as Robert McKeon, gradually welcomed her back into the fold of thinkers and scholars.[3] (Bellow, ever combative, couldn't resist a belated gibe in *Mr. Sammler's Planet,* observing that "banality is the adopted disguise of a very powerful will to abolish conscience" assumed by a woman professor "making use of a tragic history to promote the foolish ideas of Weimar intellectuals.") Until 1967, she spent part of each year living in Chicago, regularly teaching Introduction to Politics, Basic Moral Propositions, and other classes in political theory, and part of the year lecturing or giving seminars on Kant, Hegel, Nietzsche, Rousseau, Marx, Spinoza, and the ancients at Yale, Cornell, Columbia, and the University of California. In 1968, she was offered a tenured professorship in the graduate faculty of the New School for Social Research in New York. She accepted the job, and her many years of incessant travel and long separations from Blücher were finally over. For the last two years of Blücher's life, they were often together and comfortable within their four walls.

With the exception of a volume of brief, powerful portraits of vanished friends and icons called *Men in Dark Times,* Arendt published no new books for a period of seven years. Her *Men,* which included Isak Dinesen and Rosa Luxemburg as well as Karl Jaspers, Walter Benjamin, and Bertolt Brecht, were primarily figures who had lived at the center of the twentieth century's political and moral catastrophes and yet managed to cast streams of light by virtue of their gifts and courage. She also edited and finally saw printed a collection of the manuscripts of Walter Benjamin that she and Blücher had brought to America in 1941; the collection was fittingly entitled *Illuminations.* (A second book of Benjamin's essays, called *Reflections,* was published in 1978.) In her own essays in *The New Yorker* and the *New York Review of Books,* as well as in speeches and graduate seminars, she carefully elaborated an important, if sometimes buried, theme of her earlier work that had become increasingly important to her since *Rahel Varnhagen*: the differences for freedom of thought between the ancient field of political discourse and the necessary but less exalting modern "social" sphere — that is, between open discussion of rights and responsibilities among free people, in a forum where new ideas and patterns of greatness can spontaneously emerge, and a more predictable preoccupation with matters of social and material welfare, in which action is limited to managing the distribution of existing goods and resources. She wrote of America's Founding Fathers as exemplary men of action who, while fighting to secure their political rights, had discovered something entirely new, self-government, which tradition had not handed down. On the other hand, she remained conscious that the quest for political rights — in racially tense America as in anti-Semitic Germany — can cause personal pain, particularly for children. "Psychologically, the situation of being unwanted (a typically social predicament) is more difficult to bear than outright persecution (a political predicament) because personal pride is involved. By pride, I [mean] that untaught and natural feeling of identity with whatever we happen to be by accident of birth," she noted in a letter to *Dissent,* in an exchange of opinions about the integration of the public schools in Little Rock and elsewhere.[4] She thought that pariah status ought not to be forced upon the young.

Her hope for the world lay in "natality," "the miracle that

saves the world,"[5] she wrote, by which she meant the unimaginable possibilities that attend every human birth and must be safeguarded until they can reach full flower. "The beginning is also a god; so long as he dwells among men, he saves all things," she noted, quoting Plato in her 1971 tribute to Martin Heidegger upon his eightieth birthday.[6] And as she would write poignantly in her last book, *The Life of the Mind,* published after her death in 1978:

> In this world which we enter, appearing from a nowhere, and from which we disappear into a nowhere, *Being and Appearing coincide.* . . . Seen from the viewpoint of the spectators to whom [a human life] appears and from whose view it finally disappears, each individual life, its growth and decline, is a developmental process in which an entity unfolds itself in an upward movement until all its properties are fully exposed; this phase is followed by a period of standstill — its bloom or epiphany, as it were — which in turn is succeeded by the downward movement of disintegration that is terminated by complete disappearance.[7]

The human soul is born to make an appearance on a public stage, Arendt seemed to have concluded in her later years, and to become most vibrantly itself in a shared world. For her, authenticity did not require withdrawal from noisy modernity into the solitude of Being, as it did for Heidegger, but neither did it permit taking action without standing back and thinking about "what is."[8] And in her later years *what is* always encompassed the point of view of people different, even alien, from oneself.

"Thoughtlessness" was the crime of which Arendt found Eichmann guilty in her book, and some of her finest late essays and lectures were explorations of what is meant by thought. Although a thinking self cannot take shape except in solitude, she mused, it must be a populated solitude. First, one has to think in dialogue with oneself and reach an agreement with one-self. "The principle of agreement with oneself is very old," she wrote in an essay called "The Crisis in Culture," collected in *Between Past and Future*. "[I]t was actually discovered by Socrates, whose central tenet, as formulated by Plato, is contained in the sentence: 'Since I am one, it is better for me to disagree with the whole world than to be in disagreement with myself.'" The idea that one must conduct oneself in such a way that "the principle of your action can become a general law"—Kant's categorical imperative—"is based upon the necessity for rational thought to agree with itself. The thief, for instance, is actually contradicting himself, for he cannot wish that the principle of his action, stealing other people's property, should become a general law; such a law would immediately deprive him of his own acquisition."[9] She called this mode of thinking the "two-in-one," and it was a kind of thinking that Eichmann failed to do.[10]

There was also a second kind of thinking, she reflected, one that formed the basis of all sound judgment. In order to know "what is" and take judicious action, one must also think with a host of others. She wrote:

> The power of judgment rests on a potential agreement with others, and the thinking process which is active in judging something is not, like the thought process of pure reasoning, a dialogue between me and myself, but finds itself always and primarily, even if I am quite alone in making up my mind, in an anticipated communication with others with whom I know I must finally come to some agreement. From this potential agreement judgment derives its specific validity. This means, on the one hand, that such judgment must liberate itself from the "subjective private conditions," that is, from the idiosyncrasies which naturally determine the outlook of each individual in his privacy and are legitimate as long as they are only privately held opinions, but which are not fit to enter the market place, and lack all validity in the public realm.[11]

Eichmann could not do this either. Nor, perhaps, could almost anyone who had not the heart and mind to defy conventional wisdom, which tends to believe that it is right. Arendt, after Eichmann, became a master of such thinking.

For this reason and others, events in Vietnam-era American public life rattled and distressed her. The assassination of John F. Kennedy and its dreadful aftermath — the Warren Commission, competing conspiracy theories, and the increasingly bold lies of succeeding political entities — caused her to fear, with foresight, the end of an era of public spiritedness and honest discourse in American politics. She devoted the last two books published in her lifetime, *On Violence* and *Crises of the Republic,* to a warning against government power and political lies. Side by side with her students, she protested the Vietnam War and military research by institutions of higher learning on which it partly depended, but she drew the line at student action against colleges and universities themselves. At their best, universities were "refuges of truth." They were "exposed to all the dangers arising from social and political power," she argued in the essay "Truth and Politics," which appeared in *The New Yorker* in 1967.[12] Refuges of truth require protection from popular passions and opinions, even seemingly righteous ones. She was corresponding with Heidegger fairly regularly in these years. If while composing the essay she recalled the woeful passions that had ruled his rectorship in 1933, she did not say so. She had stopped writing explicitly about the Nazi era. But the problems of "otherness," ill judgment, and attendant evil that the Nazi era brought into being underlay all her late writings, just as "the basis of her teaching, the source of everything that followed, was the unprecedented event of totalitarianism," which had "exploded the categories of traditional political thought," as one of her New School students, Jerome Kohn, recalled.[13]

Students venerated her for her intensity and flair, as well as for her warmth and erudition. She had the effect on them that

Heidegger had had on her: They could *see* her thinking. "She was a tsunami of thought," recalled one.[14] Her classes were crowded, not only with those who were officially enrolled but also with former students, visiting professors, and stray intellectual passersby who elbowed their way into her classrooms in Chicago and New York City to hear what she might have to say about Kant, the existentialists, the philosophy of politics, or the history of the will. Many sat on the floor as she spoke, often haltingly at first, from behind an old-fashioned lectern, and afterward she invited and answered questions. She struck some of her listeners as "shy, modest, and strangely vulnerable." She was "never quite convinced she deserved all the attention she received," one recalled. Yet her gaiety, wit, and passion, her vast knowledge of texts, her "testy impatience," reliance on common sense, and joy in imparting her hard-earned wisdom to others made her one of the great teachers of the time.[15]

Her observations about the divisions between public life and private contemplation reflected a growing division in herself. Her appetite for intimate friendships and privacy increased as she got older. She especially valued the time she spent alone with Blücher. During summers, when they were free from teaching duties, they left the hot—and, by the late 1960s, dangerous and chaotic—city for a rented cabin in the woods at Palenville, New York, or an airy boardinghouse in Tegna, Switzerland, northwest of Locarno in the foothills of the Alps. There they were sometimes joined by Mary McCarthy and her fourth husband, James West, or Anne Mendelssohn, or Edna Brocke and Brocke's new husband, a German professor of Jewish studies, and Blücher's Berlin sidekick Robert Gilbert. By 1967, both Arendt and Blücher were growing frail, and they no longer enjoyed the kind of large summer house parties McCarthy and others had organized on Cape Cod in the 1950s. At most, they paid quiet visits to Jaspers in Basel and McCarthy in Maine. At home in New York, in their apartment on the Hudson, they spent quiet, convivial evenings with old friends such as Paul Tillich and Hans Jonas, with whom she gradually made peace in the wake of the Eichmann uproar, or newer ones such as W. H. Auden, who won Arendt's friendship on publishing an exuberant review of *The Human Condition*[16] and whose poetry she deeply admired and often recited from memory or quoted in her work. She dedicated "Thinking and Moral Considerations," her final, oblique reflection on the Eichmann trial, to Auden. He proposed marriage to her once she became a widow in 1970.[17] She demurred, with a certain amount of guilt concerning her "refusal to take care of him."[18] But she had known him for only a decade, and his housekeeping was notoriously bad.

Karl Jaspers died in February 1969 at the age of eighty-six. In some ways, he had been Hannah's only dependable parent, never failing to recognize her in her distinctiveness, as both Paul and Martha Arendt had at one time or another done, and always at the ready to discuss and even be persuaded by her least conventional ideas. "You have reached a point where many people no longer understand you," he told her kindly in the aftermath of *Eichmann in Jerusalem.* "'The Girl from Faraway,'" he added: "You are experiencing that in a new way. It strikes me as a beginning."[19] She flew to Basel to deliver the eulogy at his memorial service. The eulogy was short. Its theme — one of the constant themes of her last years — was the importance of appearance. "Every so often someone emerges among us who realizes human existence in an exemplary way and is the bodily incarnation of something that we would otherwise know only as a concept or ideal," she had said a decade earlier. "Because his existence was governed by the passion for light itself, he was able to be like a light in the darkness glowing from some hidden source of luminosity."[20] Now, she said, "A relationship with the dead one — this must be learned." She found it a hard lesson to master.

Throughout the 1960s, Blücher was periodically ill and often depressed and anxious with what doctors described as "neu-rological symptoms" of the ruptured aneurism that had felled him briefly in 1961. Heartbroken and angry over the attacks on Arendt after the publication of *Eichmann in Jerusalem,* he had been seriously ill once again in the fall of 1963. "Life without him would be unthinkable," Arendt wrote to Mary McCarthy that September.[21] In the spring of 1968, he suffered a series of mild heart attacks. He returned to teaching in the fall, giving his last lecture at Bard in December 1968, on the responsibility that the old and the young owe to each other. "There is a rea-son for respecting those who have brought you into the world regardless of what you might think of the world," he told his students, and, "There are no monsters, except those set into the world by men." His remarks were "warnings sent across genera-tions, to young people impatient for change, that the world was far more complex than they had previously imagined," recalled a student who was present at the lecture.[22] He died on Octo-ber 31, 1970, of a massive heart attack. "How am I to live now?" Arendt asked the friends who gathered to grieve with her. She considered giving him a Jewish burial service, although he was not Jewish, because it was what she remembered Martha having done for Paul Arendt upon his death in October 1913. Instead, there were services in a nondenominational chapel in New York and at Bard, where he was buried.[23] Scores of friends and stu-dents attended, and then Arendt was left alone.

To Heidegger, she wrote of Blücher's death:

Between two people, sometimes, how rarely, a world grows. It is then one's homeland; in any case, it was the only homeland we were willing to recognize. This tiny microworld where you can always escape from the world, and which disintegrates when the other has gone away.... I go now and am quite calm and think: *away.*[24]

She reconciled herself to Israel. When a Hebrew edition of *Eichmann in Jerusalem* was published in 1966, she wrote to Jaspers, "I think the war between me and the Jews is over."[25] In 1967, soon after the end of the Six-Day War, she visited the Fuersts and Edna Brocke, and they took her to several battle sites, including Gaza and Hebron. "It was extremely interesting for the whole family to see how she really faced [the reality of an embattled Israel] for the first time. But she didn't write it down,"[26] that is, except to confide in a letter to McCarthy that "any real catastrophe in Israel would affect me more deeply than almost anything else."[27] She visited again after Blücher's death. "She became much more attached, not only to us as family but also to the Jewish cause," Brocke recalled. Arendt's family in Israel had long disapproved of Blücher, just as her mother had.

They disapproved equally of her lasting friendship with Heidegger, even without knowing that he had been her lover. Brocke saw Arendt for the last time in July 1975, in Marbach, Germany, where she had traveled to organize Karl Jaspers's literary papers. She stayed in Marbach for four weeks. Brocke and her husband took Arendt to the railway station to board a train for Freiburg. "She was going to Heidegger," Brocke recalled. "And I asked her, is it really necessary? And she told me — I still hear it — 'Fröschlein (little frog), there are things stronger than men.' Those were the last words I heard from her."[28] She found Heidegger to be very old. It seemed to her that many of her oldest friends were suddenly very old.[29]

Hannah Arendt died of a heart attack on December 4, 1975. After dinner with Salo Baron and his wife, Jeannette, "She sank back into her living-room chair where she had settled to serve after-dinner coffee," wrote her friend and former student Elisabeth Young-Bruehl.[30] She lost consciousness and couldn't be revived. Her ashes are buried at Bard, beside those of Blücher, with a simple stone recalling the dates of her life.

Three hundred mourners from two continents gathered

for her memorial service on December 8, in the chapel where
Blücher had been memorialized five years earlier.[31] "Things
looked different after she had looked at them," Hans Jonas said.
"Thinking was her passion, and thinking for her was a moral activity." Jonas recalled their first acquaintance as fellow students
at Marburg in 1924. "Shy and withdrawn, with striking, beautiful features and lonely eyes, she stood immediately out as 'exceptional,' as 'unique.' . . . Brightness of intellect was no rare article there," he continued. "But here was an intensity, an inner
direction, an instinct for quality, a groping for essence, a prob-
ing for depth, which cast a magic about her. One felt an absolute determination to be herself, with the toughness to carry it
through in the face of great vulnerability." She did not believe
that "truth is to be had for these days," but did believe in the
"incessant, always temporary trying for the face of it which the
present condition happens to turn toward us. Even her errors
were more worthwhile than the verities of lesser minds."[32] Robert Lowell spoke passionately of her admirable "voyage of wisdom" in an age that often seemed merely dry and dusty.[33] Edna
Brocke read Psalm 90 in Hebrew, which begins, "Lord, thou
hast been our dwelling place in all generations." Speaking last,
Mary McCarthy evoked the physical presence of her best friend.
"She was a beautiful woman, alluring, seductive, feminine," Mc-
Carthy said, "[with] small, fine hands, charming ankles, elegant
feet." Arendt's eyes sparkled and were starry when expressing excitement, were dark and remote when she was deep in thought.
What was most theatrical about such a shy woman, McCarthy
said, was a kind of "spontaneous power of being seized by an
idea, an emotion, a presentiment." She was the only person
Mary McCarthy had ever seen think.[34]

In *Men in Dark Times*, Hannah Arendt wrote what could
almost have been her own eulogy when she elaborated on the
twists and turns, the oddities and courage, in the life of her deceased friend Waldemar Gurion, a fellow émigré from Nazi

Germany. "He was an extraordinary and extraordinarily strange man," she wrote, adding, "He remained a stranger and whenever he came [to visit] it was as though he arrived from nowhere. But when he died, his friends mourned him as though a member of the family had gone and left them behind."[35]

If thoughtful men and women mourned the loss of Hannah Arendt, it was at least in part because in her great books — *The Origins of Totalitarianism, The Human Condition,* and *Eichmann in Jerusalem* — as in almost all her works, she remained something of a stranger, willing to examine the world from the point of view of an outsider, even in dark and dangerous times.

Acknowledgments

I am indebted to the librarians and archivists of the Hannah Arendt Papers at the Library of Congress in Washington, D.C.; the Columbia University Rare Book and Manuscript Library and Center for Oral History; the Berg Collection of the New York Public Library; the Heinrich Blücher Archive at Bard College; the archival collections of the Leo Baeck Institute; Yad Vashem; and the Hoover Institution Library and Archives at Stanford University. I owe special thanks to Glenn Horowitz and Sarah Funke Butler of Glenn Horowitz Bookseller, Inc., in New Canaan and New York, who made the firm's most interesting private collection of Arendt-related correspondence, lecture notes, and other original documents available to me, along with a comfortable working place. Thanks also to Jay Barksdale of the Allen Room at the New York Public Library and to the staff of the New York Society Library, where I have spent many hours working in the stacks and the fifth-floor writing rooms.

Thanks to Peter Baehr, Roger Berkowitz, Richard Bernstein, Ann Birstein, Edna Brocke, Michael Denneny, Wolfgang Heuer, Beryl Lang, Jerome Kohn, and Jean Yarbrough, among others, who gave me their time, knowledge, and guidance. Any errors of fact or judgment are my own.

I benefitted from attending a number of workshops and conferences, including "Exercising Judgment in Ethics, Politics, and the Law: Hannah Arendt's *Eichmann in Jerusalem: A Re-*

port on the Banality of Evil, Fifty Years Later," with Seyla Ben-habib, Peter Gordon, and Dana Villa at Wesleyan University; "The Banality of Evil: Death of a Legend," with Richard Wolin and Jeffrey Herf at the Graduate Center of the City University of New York; and "The Black Notebooks (1931–1941)," a panel discussion with Peter Trawny, Roger Berkowitz, and Babette Babich at the Goethe Institute in New York. I also attended helpful lectures and panel discussions sponsored by the excellent Hannah Arendt Center at Bard College, founded and led by Roger Berkowitz.

I am grateful to the Research Internship Program of the School of the Arts at Columbia University, which provided me with an able research assistant, Zach Hindin, at the beginning of my work on this book. My thanks go to Zach and to the program director, Patricia O'Toole.

Finally, warm thanks to my literary agent and friend, Amanda Urban, and to my terrific editor, James Atlas.

Notes

1 Bertold Brecht, "To Posterity," quoted in Hannah Arendt, *Men in Dark Times* (New York: Harcourt, Brace & World, 1968).

1: Eichmann in Jerusalem

1 "Eichmann Was Outrageously Stupid," interview with Hannah Arendt by Joachim Fest, November 9, 1964, translated by Andrew Brown, in *Hannah Arendt, The Last Interview and Other Conversations* (Brooklyn, NY: Melville House, 2013), 43.

2 Arendt to Karl Jaspers, July 20, 1963, in Lotte Kohler and Hans Saner, eds., *Correspondence: 1926–1969*, trans. Robert Kimber and Rita Kimber (New York: Harcourt Brace Jovanovich, 1992), 511.

3 "Killer of 6,000,000," *New York Times*, May 26, 1960.

4 Hannah Arendt, *Eichmann in Jerusalem: A Report on the Banality of Evil* (New York: Penguin Books, 1963, 1964), 276 (hereafter cited as *EIJ*).

5 Ibid., 123.

6 Leo Mindlin, "During the Week . . . ," *Jewish Floridian*, March 15, 1963; also see "Eichmann in Jerusalem — Can One Know the Whole Truth?" *Newsweek*, June 17, 1963.

7 Arendt to Mary McCarthy, September 16, 1963, in Brightman, ed., *Between Friends: The Correspondence of Hannah Arendt and Mary McCarthy 1949–1975* (New York: Harcourt Brace, 1995), 146.

8 Israel was founded on May 14, 1948.

9 David Cesarani, *Eichmann: His Life and Crimes* (London: W. Heine-mann, 2004), 255.

10 Deborah E. Lipstadt, *The Eichmann Trial* (New York: Schocken, 2011).

11 Edna Brocke, interview with the author, April 18, 2013.

12 "Eichmann Trial to Be Seen on TV," *New York Times,* November 14, 1960.

13 "The Eichmann Trial — Proceedings: The 15 Charges," *The Trial of Adolf Eichmann,* PBS Online, accessed December 13, 2014, http://remember .org/eichmann/charges.htm.

14 Reinhard Heydrich was executed by Czech assassins in Prague in 1942, and Heinrich Himmler bit into a cyanide pill when captured by the British in 1945.

15 Arendt to Jaspers, April 13, 1961, in Kohler and Saner, eds., *Correspondence,* 434.

16 "Show Trial Promised," *New York Times,* May 28, 1960. Attorney General Gideon Hausner called Eichmann Nazism's "executive arm for the extermination of the Jewish people."

17 Quoted in William L. Shirer, *The Rise and Fall of the Third Reich* (New York: Simon & Schuster, 1960), 978; *Life,* November 28 and December 5, 1960; and *EIJ,* 46 (Arendt's translation).

18 Martha Gellhorn, "Eichmann and the Private Conscience," *Atlantic Monthly,* February 1962.

19 Hannah Arendt, *The Origins of Totalitarianism* (New York: Harcourt, Brace & World, 1966), 357, 329 (hereafter cited as *OT*).

20 Arendt to Jaspers, December 2, 1960, in Kohler and Saner, eds., *Correspondence,* 409–410.

21 Jaspers to Arendt, October 14, 1960, in ibid., 267.

22 Jaspers to Arendt, December 12, 1960, in ibid., 411.

23 Arendt to Jaspers, December 2, 1960, in ibid., 409–10.

24 Arendt to Heinrich Blücher, April 26, 1961, Lotte Kohler, ed., *Within Four Walls: The Correspondence between Hannah Arendt and Heinrich Blücher, 1936–1968,* trans. Peter Constantine (New York: Harcourt, 2000), 361.

25 Arendt to Blücher, April 26, 1961, in Kohler, ed., *Within Four Walls,* 361.

26 Arendt to Jaspers, December 23, 1960, in Kohler and Saner, eds., *Correspondence,* 414.

27 Lawrence Fellows, "Israel Determined to Try Gestapo Man, Despite Possible Domestic Repercussions and Foreign Protests over Method of Capture," *New York Times,* June 12, 1960.

28 Arendt to Jaspers, December 23, 1960, in Kohler and Saner, eds., *Correspondence,* 417.

29 The Trial of Adolf Eichmann, District Court Sessions, Volume I, the Nizkor Project online, http://www.nizkor.org/hweb/people/e/eichmann -adolf/transcripts/Sessions/index-o1.html (hereafter cited as Nizkor).

30 *EIJ,* 5.

31 Cesarani, *Eichmann,* 251.

32 *EIJ,* 207

33 Arendt to Jaspers, December 23, 1960, in Kohler and Saner, eds., *Correspondence,* 416.

34 *EIJ,* 124.

35 Arendt to Blücher, May 8, 1961, in Kohler, ed., *Within Four Walls,* 366–67.

36 *EIJ,* 8.

37 *EIJ,* 48.

38 William Barrett, *The Truants: Adventures among the Intellectuals* (Garden City, NY: Anchor Press/Doubleday, 1982), 103.

39 These include almost 900 pages of Eichmann-annotated interviews conducted by the Dutch Nazi collaborator Willem Sassen, of which Arendt was familiar with only the excerpts published in *Life* plus about 70 pages of notes by Eichmann (*EIJ,* 281); "Others Have Spoken, Now I Will Speak," a 550-page memoir of which Arendt saw about 70 pages (Roger Berkowitz, letter to the editor, *New York Review of Books,* December 19, 2013); and a memoir written in the months before his execution.

40 Trial transcript, Nizkor.

41 Bettina Stangneth, *Eichmann before Jerusalem: The Unexamined Life of a Mass Murderer* (New York: Alfred A. Knopf, 2014), 209.

42 "[H]is was obviously also no case of insane hatred of Jews, of fanatical anti-Semitism or indoctrination of any kind," she wrote (*EIJ,* 26).

43 "Eichmann Tells His Own Damning Story," pt. 1, *Life,* November 28, 1960.

44 They also acquitted him of committing crimes against European Jews

with intent to destroy the Jewish people in the period before he learned of Hitler's decision to adopt the Final Solution.

45 Stangneth, *Eichmann before Jerusalem,* 365.

46 *EIJ,* 54.

47 Ibid., 32.

48 Ibid., 287.

49 Jaspers to Arendt, December 13, 1963, in Kohler and Saner, eds., *Correspondence,* 542.

50 Bertolt Brecht, notes for *The Resistible Rise of the Man of Arturo Ui* (London: Bloomsbury Methuen Drama, 2013).

51 Arendt to Jaspers, December 1, 1963, in Kohler and Saner, eds., *Correspondence,* 539.

52 University of Chicago lecture notes dated October 30, 1963, Hannah Arendt Papers, Manuscript Division, Library of Congress, Washington, D.C.

53 "He was not stupid," she wrote about Eichmann. "It was sheer thoughtlessness — something by no means identical with stupidity — that predisposed him to become one of the greatest criminals of that period. And if this is 'banal' and even funny, if with the best will in the world one cannot extract any diabolical or demonic profundity from Eichmann, that is still far from calling it commonplace" (*EIJ,* 287–88).

54 Draft letter to Samuel Grafton, October 30, 1963, Hannah Arendt Papers, Library of Congress.

55 University of Chicago lecture notes, Hannah Arendt Papers, Library of Congress.

56 *OT,* 317.

57 Alfred Kazin, *New York Jew* (New York: Knopf, 1978), 196.

58 Irving Howe, *A Margin of Hope* (San Diego, CA: Harcourt Brace Jovanovich, 1982), 274.

59 *EIJ,* 7.

60 Ibid., 93.

61 Ibid., 116: "As Eichmann told it, the most potent factor in the soothing of his own conscience was the simple fact that he could see no one, no one at all, who actually was against the Final Solution."

62 The quote came from and was attributed to Raul Hilberg's 1961 book *The Destruction of the European Jews.* The indented passage is from Han-

nah Arendt, "Eichmann in Jerusalem," pt. 3, *The New Yorker,* March 2, 1963. She added, "The few who tried to hide or to escape were rounded up by a special Jewish police force. As far as Eichmann could see, no one protested, no one refused to cooperate" (*EIJ,* 115).

63 *EIJ,* 125.

64 Ibid., 117.

65 Ibid.,5.

66 Ibid., 279.

67 Arendt to Gertrud and Karl Jaspers, March 31, 1962, in Kohler and Saner, eds., *Correspondence,* 473.

68 Quoted in Elisabeth Young-Bruehl, *Hannah Arendt: For Love of the World* (New Haven, CT: Yale University Press), 349.

69 Arendt to Jaspers, July 20, 1963, in Kohler and Saner, eds., *Correspondence,* 510.

70 Hannah Arendt Papers, Library of Congress.

71 Mindlin, "During the Week . . ."

72 Michael A. Musmanno, "Man with an Unspotted Conscience," *New York Times,* May 19, 1963.

73 Marie Syrkin, "Hannah Arendt: The Clothes of the Empress," *Dissent,* Autumn 1963.

74 Ibid.

75 Mary McCarthy, "The Hue and Cry," *Partisan Review,* Winter 1964.

76 Marie Syrkin, "More on Eichmann," *Partisan Review,* Spring 1964.

77 Howe, *A Margin of Hope,* 274.

78 Irving Spiegel, "Hausner Criticizes Book on Eichmann," *New York Times,* May 20, 1963.

79 Jacob Robinson, *And the Crooked Shall Be Made Straight: The Eichmann Trial, the Jewish Catastrophe, and Hannah Arendt's Narrative* (New York: Macmillan, 1965).

80 Hannah Arendt, "'The Formidable Dr. Robinson': A Reply," *New York Review of Books,* January 20, 1966.

81 Arendt to Jaspers, October 20, 1963, in Kohler and Saner, eds., *Correspondence,* 522.

82 Arendt to Jaspers, August 9, 1963, in ibid., 516.

83 Arendt to Jaspers, October 20, 1963, in ibid., 521.

84 Arendt to Jaspers, October 20, 1963, in ibid., 524.

85 Arendt to Jaspers, April 13, 1961, in Kohler and Saner, eds., *Correspondence*, 435.

86 "Edna Brock on Hannah Arendt," video interview, 1:01:12, Hannah Arendt Center for Politics and Humanities at Bard College, April 16, 2012, http://www.bard.edu/hannaharendtcenter/video/.

87 Gershom Scholem to Arendt, June 23, 1963, in Gershom Scholem, *A Life in Letters, 1914–1982* (Cambridge, MA: Harvard University Press, 2002), 398.

88 Hannah Arendt, *The Jew as Pariah: Jewish Identity and Politics in the Modern Age*, ed. Ron H. Feldman (New York: Grove Press, 1978), 240–51.

89 Edna Brocke, interview, April 18, 2013.

90 Daniel Bell, *The End of Ideology: On the Exhaustion of Political Idea in the Fifties* (Cambridge, MA: Harvard University Press, 1962), quoted in Young-Bruehl, *Hannah Arendt*, 365.

91 Scholem to Daniel Bell, December 1980, in Scholem, *A Life in Letters*, 487–88.

92 Arendt to Gertrud and Karl Jaspers, February 8, 1963, in Kohler and Saner, eds., *Correspondence*, 499.

93 Edna Brocke, interview, April 18, 2013.

94 Reported without attribution in Young-Bruehl, *Hannah Arendt*, 353.

2: Death of the Father

1 *Hannah Arendt: The Last Interview*, 34.

2 *Hannah Arendt: The Last Interview*, 16.

3 Notes from "Personal Responsibility under Dictatorship," Glenn Horowitz Archive of Rare Books and Papers, New York.

4 Shmuel Feiner, *Moses Mendelssohn: Sage of Modernity* (New Haven, CT: Yale University Press, 2010).

5 Quoted from translation of Gaus interview in "14.10.1906: Birth of Hannah Arendt," Today in History, accessed December 16, 2014, http://www.today-in-history.de/index.php?what=thmanu&manu_id=1612&tag=14&monat=10&year=2012&dayisset=1&lang=en.

6 Arendt had nine sets of aunts and uncles on both sides and twelve cousins; in 1975, she had one aunt by marriage and five cousins, including Edna Brocke's father, Ernst Fuerst; Young-Bruehl, *Hannah Arendt*, xlix.

7   Ibid., 19.

8   In a reminiscence of Lotte Kohler by Elisabeth Young-Bruehl, Young-Bruehl wrote that Kohler once told her of recounting to Hannah a dream she, Kohler, had. "[Hannah], too, had a recurrent dream, and one uncannily like Lotte's. As a little girl, she was standing alone in the road near her family home when, down the road, came a wagon which her father was driving. She waited with tremendous excitement for him to climb down and take her in his arms. Soon, however, he got back onto the wagon and drove away. The only way she could get him to come back was to dream the dream again." Young-Bruehl on Lotte Kohler, in "Lotte Kohler, in Memoriam," *Who's Afraid of Social Democracy?* (blog), May 30, 2011.

9   Young-Bruehl, *Hannah Arendt,* 23.

10 "The Shadows," in Ursula Ludz, ed., *Letters, 1925–1975: Hannah Arendt and Martin Heidegger,* trans. Andrew Shields (Orlando, FL: Harcourt, 2004), 13–14.

11 Hans Jonas, Brian Fox, and Richard Wolin, "Hannah Arendt: An Intimate Portrait," *New England Review* 27, no. 2 (2006): 133–42.

12 Hannah Arendt, "'What Remains? The Language Remains': A Conversation with Günter Gaus," in *The Portable Hannah Arendt,* ed. Peter Baehr (New York: Penguin, 2000), 8.

13 Young-Bruehl, *Hannah Arendt,* 32. Also see *Hannah Arendt: The Last Interview,* 14–15: She was fourteen when she read Kant, Jaspers, and Kierkegaard.

14 Young-Bruehl, *Hannah Arendt,* 8.

15 Ibid., 71.

16 *Hannah Arendt: The Last Interview,* 12.

17 Isaiah Friedman, *Germany, Turkey, and Zionism, 1897–1918* (Oxford: Clarendon Press, 1977), 129.

18 Elisabeth Albanis, *German-Jewish Cultural Identity from 1900 to the Aftermath of the First World War: A Comparative Study of Moritz Goldstein, Julius Bab, and Ernst Lissauer* (Tübingen, Germany: Niemeyer, 2002), 30. "The increase in the immigration of Jews from the East after 1881 was another factor in cultural Judeophobia among non-Jewish . . . Germans. Following the expulsion of Russian Jews in the years following 1881, by 1910 79,000 of Germany's 615,000 Jews were of foreign extraction. . . ."

19 *Hannah Arendt: The Last Interview,* 14.

20 Arendt to Jaspers, September 7, 1952, in Kohler and Saner, eds., *Correspondence*, 197.

3: First Love

1   Hannah Arendt, "Heidegger at Eighty," *The New York Review of Books*, October 21, 1971.
2   "I will be lecturing in room 11 again; do you know what that means?" Heidegger to Arendt, April 24, 1925, in Ludz, ed., *Letters*, 18.
3   See opening poem, November 1924, in ibid., 68.
4   Described by Rüdiger Safranski in *Martin Heidegger: Between Good and Evil* (Cambridge, MA: Harvard University Press, 1998), 131, and Elzbieta Ettinger in *Hannah Arendt/Martin Heidegger* (New Haven, CT: Yale University Press, 1995), 11, among other sources.
5   Safranski, *Martin Heidegger*, 100.
6   Hannah Arendt, "Martin Heidegger at Eighty": "There was hardly more than a name," Arendt wrote in tribute half a century after meeting Heidegger, "but the name traveled all over Germany like the rumor of the hidden king."
7   Safranski, *Martin Heidegger*, 94–95.
8   Arendt, "Martin Heidegger at Eighty." She went on: "[T]he cultural treasures of the past, believed to be dead, are being made to speak, in the course of which it turns out that they propose things altogether different from the familiar, worn-out trivialities they had been presumed to say. There exists a teacher; one can perhaps learn to think."
9   Hans-Georg Gadamer, *Heidegger's Ways* (Albany: State University of New York Press, 1994), 17–18.
10 Heidegger's lectures, 1923–28, from a listing of Heidegger's complete works online at http://www.beyng.com/hb/gesamt.html#18\.
11 Karl Löwith, *Mein Leben in Deutschland vor und nach 1933*, translated in Ettinger, *Hannah Arendt/Martin Heidegger*, 11.
12 Ludz, ed., *Letters*, 223, note 1 (pertaining to letter 14).
13 Safranski, *Martin Heidegger*, 130.
14 Young-Bruehl, *Hannah Arendt*, 3. In 1964, Arendt told Günter Gaus that she decided on philosophy at age fourteen.

15 Romano Guardini was later fired for publicly reminding the Nazi Party that Jesus was a Jew.
16 Von Wiese joined the National Socialist Party in 1933.
17 Benno von Wiese, quoted in Safranski, *Martin Heidegger,* 137.
18 Ibid., 137.
19 Babette Babich, "Angels, the Space of Time, and Apocalyptic Blindness: On Günther Anders' Endzeit–Endtime," *Ethics & Politics* 15 (2013): 144–74.
20 Michael Denneny, interview with the author, March 9, 2009.
21 Arendt to Blücher, May 24, 1952, Kohler, ed., *Within Four Walls,* 177.
22 Peter Trawny, Roger Berkowitz, and Babette Babich, "The Black Notebooks (1931–1941)" (panel discussion, Goethe Institute, New York, April 8, 2014). Trawny is the director of the Martin Heidegger Institute at the University of Wuppertal in Germany and the editor of Heidegger's Black Notebooks (some of which were published as *Schwarze Hefte* for the first time in the spring of 2014).
23 Heidegger to the Ministry of Education, October 1929, cited by Ettinger, *Hannah Arendt/Martin Heidegger,* 37. The letter was sent after he visited Arendt and her new husband, Günther Stern, in Frankfurt.
24 Trawny, Berkowitz, and Babich, "The Black Notebooks."
25 Heidegger to Arendt, February 21, 1925, in Ludz, ed., *Letters,* 3.
26 Heidegger to Arendt, February 21, 1925, in ibid., 4.
27 Heidegger to Arendt, February 27, 1925, in ibid., 6.
28 Arendt reported this to Blücher after a visit to the Heideggers in 1950: Kohler, ed., *Within Four Walls,* 128.
29 Heidegger to Arendt, July 1, 1925, in Ludz, ed., *Letters,* 26. Also: "Do you want to come and see me this Sunday evening? Come around nine o'clock!" (27).
30 They also read Thomas Mann's new novel *The Magic Mountain* together. Ibid., 292 and May 21/22,1925, 22.
31 Arendt to Heidegger, undated (April 1925), in Ludz, ed., *Letters,* 16.
32 Heidegger, *Denkerfahrungen* [Thought Experiences], *1910–1976,* translated in Safranski, *Martin Heidegger,* 3.
33 Ibid., 137.
34 Heidegger to Arendt, June 22, 1925, in Ludz, ed., *Letters,* 25.

35 Ibid., 228, note 1 (pertaining to letter 31).

36 Arendt to Heidegger, Summer 1925, in ibid., 300.

37 Safranski, *Martin Heidegger,* 143.

38 Heidegger to Arendt, January 10, 1926, in Ludz, ed., *Letters,* 40–41.

39 Arendt to Heidegger, February 9, 1950, in ibid., 60.

40 Ettinger, *Hannah Arendt/Martin Heidegger,* 29, 37; Kohler, ed., *Within Four Walls,* 128.

41 Bob Sandmeyer, "Husserl, Edmund (1859–1938): A Biography," Husserl Page, accessed December 17, 2014, http://www.husserlpage.com/hus_bio.html.

42 Arendt to Heidegger, April 22, 1928, in Ludz, ed., *Letters,* 50.

43 According to Roger Berkowitz, based on Stern's memoir, *Die Kirschenschlact: Dialoge mit Hannah Arendt* (The Cherry Battle: Dialogues with Hannah Arendt), "they met in Martin Heidegger's lecture hall where they both heard lectures on Hegel's *Logic* and participated in a seminar on Kant's *Critique of Pure Reason.* Arendt, at the time in love with their professor, had little time for Anders (who went by his family name Günther Stern). Five years later, in 1929, they met again at a masked ball in Berlin" ("The Cherry Battle," Hannah Arendt Center, posted February 13, 2012, http://www.hannaharendtcenter.org/?p=4302).

44 Heidegger to Arendt, October 18, 1925, in Ludz, ed., *Letters,* 37–38.

45 Arendt to Heidegger, September, 1929, in ibid., 51.

46 Arendt to Heidegger, September 30, 1929, in ibid., 51.

47 Arendt to Blücher, August 24, 1936, in Kohler, ed., *Within Four Walls,* 21.

48 Hannah Arendt, *Rahel Varnhagen: The Life of a Jewess* (London: Leo Baeck Institute, 1957) (hereafter cited as *RV*).

49 *Hannah Arendt: The Last Interview,* 18.

50 Arendt to Blücher, August 12, 1936, Kohler, ed., *Within Four Walls,* 10.

51 *Hannah Arendt: The Last Interview,* 20.

52 *RV,* 254.

53 Ibid., 256.

54 "Conscious pariah" is a phrase used by Bernard Lazare, first heard by Arendt in conversation with Kurt Blumenfeld.

55 Heidegger to Arendt, Winter 1932/33, in Ludz, ed., *Letters,* 52–53.

56 Safranski, *Martin Heidegger,* 240–1.

57 Arendt to Jaspers, July 9, 1946, in Kohler and Saner, eds., *Correspondence*, 48.
58 Heidegger's rector's address, May 1933, quoted in Safranski, *Martin Heidegger*, 245.
59 George Steiner, *Martin Heidegger* (New York: Viking Press, 1979), 82–83.
60 *RV,* 171.
61 *EIJ,* 49.
62 Martin Heidgger, *Discourse on Thinking* (New York: Harper & Row, 1959). The book was published two years before the Eichmann trial.
63 Heidegger to Arendt, May 13, 1925, in Ludz, ed., *Letters*, 21.
64 *OT,* 301.
65 Ettinger, *Hannah Arendt/Martin Heidegger,* 15.
66 *Hannah Arendt: The Last Interview,* 18.
67 Ibid. Omitted between these sentences: "I never forgot that."

4: We Refugees

1 Hannah Arendt, "We Refugees," *The Jewish Writings*, 274.
2 *Hannah Arendt: The Last Interview,* 9.
3 Reported without attribution in Young-Bruehl, *Hannah Arendt*, 102.
4 *Hannah Arendt: The Last Interview,* 20.
5 Ibid., 9–10.
6 Arendt to Blücher, August 24, 1936, Kohler, ed., *Within Four Walls*, 20.
7 *Hannah Arendt: The Last Interview,* 18, 20.
8 A writer whose novels, along with those of Thomas Mann, Erich Maria Remarque, and John Dos Passos, had been burned in Berlin's Opera Square in May 1933.
9 Howard Eiland and Michael W. Jennings, *Walter Benjamin: A Critical Life* (Cambridge, MA: Belknap Press of Harvard University Press, 2014), 429.
10 Paul Johnson, *Intellectuals* (New York: Harper & Row, 1988).
11 Hannah Arendt, *Men in Dark Times,* 167.
12 Arendt, "The Jew as Pariah," *Jewish Writings*, 285.
13 In May 1934, Édouard's cousin Robert Philippe de Rothschild, then president of the Napoleonic-era French Jewish council of notables

called the Consistoire Israélite de France, which traditionally mediated between the mass of emancipated French Jews and the government, gave a speech to his council peers warning against the tide of "Polaks" and their ability to spread anti-Semitism in France; Young-Bruehl, *Hannah Arendt*, 119–20.

14 *Hannah Arendt: The Last Interview*, 30.

15 Arendt worked at the agency from 1935 to 1938. Günther Stern's sister Eva also worked there; Brian Amkraut, *Between Home and Homeland: Youth Aliyah from Nazi Germany* (Tuscaloosa: University of Alabama Press, 2006), 50.

16 "Edna Brocke on Hannah Arendt," Hannah Arendt Center; Young-Bruehl says the couple moved in 1935.

17 Edna Brocke, interview, April 18, 2013. Young-Bruehl says that Arendt earlier tried to keep Käthe Levin from joining the Zionist youth movement (*Hannah Arendt*, 100), though on the grounds that it was not sufficiently political and apparently in advance of 1933.

18 Arendt to Mary McCarthy, October 7, 1967, quoted in Young-Bruehl, *Hannah Arendt*, 139.

19 Arendt to Blücher, August 24, 1936, in Kohler, ed., *Within Four Walls*, 21.

20 According to the novelist Hermann Broch, quoted in David Laskin, *Partisans: Marriage, Politics, and Betrayal among the New York Intellectuals*, reviewed in "Hannah Arendt and Heinrich Blücher," *Louis Proyect: The Unrepentant Marxist* (blog), May 23, 2007, https://louisproyect.wordpress.com/2007/05/23/heinrich-blucher-and-hannah-arendt/.

21 Ibid.

22 See introduction to Kohler, ed., *Within Four Walls*, xvi.

23 See kidney attack, Blücher to Arendt, December 4, 1939, in ibid., 56.

24 Arendt, *Men in Dark Times*, 45.

25 His pseudonym was Heinrich Larsen.

26 Young-Bruehl, *Hannah Arendt*, 122.

27 Robert Gilbert (né Winterfield) was a filmmaker who had strummed a guitar while Blücher improvised Communist speeches on the sidewalks of Berlin.

28 This quote comes from a retrospective letter Blücher wrote to Robert Gilbert in 1960, cited by Wolfgang Hauer in a 2009 Bard Arendt Cen-

ter Conference paper called "Heinrich Blücher: The Outsider," reproduced in the online Blücher Archive at Bard College: www.bard.edu/bluecher/rel_misc/heuer_conf_sp.htm.

29 Arendt to Blücher, August 6, 1936, in Kohler, ed., *Within Four Walls*, 2.

30 Blücher to Arendt, August 12, 1936, in ibid., 10.

31 She divorced Stern in 1937.

32 "Be a good tomcat and wait patiently": Arendt to Blücher, February 13, 1937, in Kohler, ed., *Within Four Walls*, 25.

33 Arendt to Blücher, August 12, 1936, in Kohler, ed., *Within Four Walls*, 10. Including one affair I'd never heard about before.

34 Young-Bruehl, *Hannah Arendt*, 115.

35 According to Michael Wieck's book *A Childhood under Hitler and Stalin*, there were about 3,000 Jewish residents, 201 Jewish businesses, 38 doctors, and 22 lawyers remaining in the city at the time of Kristallnacht. By May 1939, a month after Martha left and when emigration no longer permitted, about 1,500 Jewish residents remained.

36 Arendt, "We Refugees," *Jewish Writings*, 267.

37 Ibid., 269.

38 Kohler, ed., *Within Four Walls*, 46, 56; Gershom Scholem, *Walter Benjamin: The Story of a Friendship* (Philadelphia: Jewish Publication Society of America, 1981), 276.

39 Blücher to Arendt, October 17, 1939, in Kohler, ed., *Within Four Walls*, 50.

40 Blücher to Arendt, November 28, 1939, in ibid., 55.

41 Blücher to Arendt, September 29, 1939, in ibid., 48.

42 Arendt to Blumenfeld, 1952, cited in Young-Bruehl, *Hannah Arendt*, 154.

43 Hannah Arendt, letter to the editor, *Midstream*, 1962.

44 According to *Wikipedia*, this deportation "could have involved setting into motion the Madagascar Plan, an initiative of Adolf Eichmann designed to transport the entire Jewish population of Europe to the island of that name. If this was the case, this deportation would be the only known attempt to carry this plan forward" ("Gurs Internment Camp," *Wikipedia*, accessed December 18, 2014, http://en.wikipedia.org/wiki/Gurs_internment_camp).

45 Arendt, "We Refugees," *Jewish Writings*, 265.

46 Heinrich Blücher, "Description of An Average Life," reproduced in the online Blücher Archive at Bard College: http://www.bard.edu/bluecher/rel_scholar.htm.

47 "W.B.," quoted in Young-Bruehl, *Hannah Arendt*, 163.

48 Jean-Michel Palmier, *Weimar in Exile: The Antifascist Emigration in Europe and America* (London and New York: Verso, 2006).

49 Arendt, "We Refugees," *Jewish Writings*, 274. The Rothschilds spent the war years in New York and returned to France in 1944.

50 "Koenigsberg," Jewish Virtual Library, accessed December 18, 2014, https://www.jewishvirtuallibrary.org/jsource/judaica/ejud_0002_0012_0_11334.html.

5: Security and Fame

1 *OT*, 372.

2 Kohler, ed., *Within Four Walls*, editor's note, 58.

3 Kazin, *New York Jew*, 183.

4 Arendt, *Jewish Writings*, 138.

5 Ibid., 137.

6 Ibid., xiv, 7, 15.

7 Ibid., 138.

8 The precursor of *Commentary*, published by the American Jewish Committee.

9 Young-Bruehl, *Hannah Arendt*, 171.

10 Blücher to Arendt, July 26, 1941, in Kohler, ed., *Within Four Walls*, 65.

11 *Hannah Arendt: The Last Interview*, 22.

12 *Aufbau*, October 25, 1941, quoted in Young-Bruehl, *Hannah Arendt*, 170.

13 Hannah Arendt, "What Is Existenz Philosophy," *Partisan Review*, Winter 1946.

14 In a footnote, she told what turned out to be an apocryphal story of Heidegger's having expelled his mentor Edmund Husserl from the Freiburg campus, a story she later recanted; in a letter to the Reverend John M. Oesterreicher, August 23, 1952 (Hannah Arendt Papers, Library of Congress), she admits she was wrong.

15 Barrett, *The Truants*, 101.

16 Ibid., 103.

17 Kazin, *New York Jew*, 196.
18 As was *Jewish Social Studies*, also founded by Salo Baron.
19 Kazin, *New York Jew*, 196.
20 David Laskin, *Partisans: Marriage, Politics, and Betrayal among the New York Intellectuals* (New York: Simon & Schuster, 2000), 26.
21 Ann Birstein, interview with the author, February 26, 2013; Ann Birstein, *What I Saw at the Fair* (New York: Welcome Rain, 2003), 125.
22 Barrett, *The Truants*, 103, 105.
23 Arendt first met McCarthy in a Murray Hill bar in 1944; they met a second time at Rahv's apartment in 1945 (Carol Brightman, ed., introduction to *Between Friends*.
24 Young-Bruehl, *Hannah Arendt*, 197.
25 Hannah Arendt, "Race-Thinking before Racism," *Review of Politics* 6, no. 1 (January 1944): 36–73.
26 Hannah Arendt, "Concerning Minorities," *Contemporary Jewish Record* 7, no. 4 (August 1944): 353–68.
27 Arendt, "The Minority Question," *Jewish Writings*, 128.
28 Hannah Arendt, "Privileged Jews," *Jewish Social Studies* 8, no. 1 (January 1946): 3–30.
29 *OT*, 64.
30 Arendt, "Privileged Jews," 9.
31 Ibid., 7.
32 Barrett, *The Truants*, 103. He added, "She could not quite get used to the idea that the worst persecutions of Jews in modern history had broken out in Germany of all countries."
33 Arendt, "Privileged Jews," 26.
34 Arendt, "The Jew as Pariah," *Jewish Writings*, 296.
35 Arendt, "We Refugees," *Jewish Writings*, 274. In "Privileged Jews," she lists these good qualities as humanity, kindness, freedom from prejudice, and rebellion against injustice.
36 Arendt, "The Jew as Pariah," *Jewish Writings*, 284.
37 Arendt, "Stefan Zweig: Jews in the World of Yesterday," *Jewish Writings*, 328.
38 *Hannah Arendt: The Last Interview*, 22–23.
39 Kazin, *New York Jew*, 196.
40 Research Staff of the Commission on European Jewish Cultural Recon-

struction, "Tentative List of Jewish Cultural Treasures in Axis-Occupied Countries," supplements, *Jewish Social Studies* 8, no. 1 (January 1946); no. 3 (July 1946); no. 10 (January 1948).

41 *OT,* 402.

42 See citations in Hannah Arendt, "The Concentration Camps," *Partisan Review,* July 1948.

43 Ibid.

44 *OT,* 458, 392.

45 Ibid., 447.

46 Arendt to Jaspers, October 31, 1948, in Kohler and Saner, eds., *Correspondence,* 117.

47 Hannah Arendt, "Achieving Agreement between Peoples in the Near East — A Basis for Jewish Politics," *Aufbau,* March 16, 1945.

48 Hannah Arendt, "To Save the Jewish Homeland: There Is Still Time," *Commentary,* May 1948, available at http://www.commentarymagazine.com/articles/to-save-the-jewish-homelandthere-is-still-time/.

49 Ibid.

50 Young-Bruehl, *Hannah Arendt,* 223.

51 "Zionism Reconsidered," which appeared in *Menorah Journal* 33 (August 1945): 162–96; Arendt, "To Save the Jewish Homeland."

52 Jacob Robinson and Hannah Arendt, "Palestine Legalities," letters to the editor, *Commentary,* June 1948, available at http://www.commentarymagazine.com/articles/palestine-legalities/.

53 Birstein, *What I Saw at the Fair,* 179; confirmed by interview with Birstein, February 26, 2013.

54 Arendt, "To Save the Jewish Homeland."

55 Introduction to Kohler and Saner, eds., *Correspondence,* x.

56 Lotte Kohler interview with David Laskin, *Partisans,* 155–56: "Martha Arendt expected Heinrich to find work, any work, but this was not for him. During those early years in New York all he did was read and read and read." Alfred Kazin interview with Laskin, *Partisans,* 159–60: "Of course Heinrich was not her intellectual equal — she was a bit of a snob and there were not many she considered her equal. But Heinrich was her partner. There was no tension between them over their intellectual standing or accomplishments. They did not compete with each other. It was not like a typical American marriage."

57 Arendt to Blücher, July 8, 1946, in Kohler, ed., *Within Four Walls*, 80.

58 Young-Bruehl, *Hannah Arendt*, 250.

59 Arendt, *Men in Dark Times*, 46–47.

60 Martha died on July 26, 1948.

61 Arendt, "We Refugees," *Jewish Writings*, 269, 270.

62 Arendt to Blücher, February 8, 1950, in Kohler, ed., *Within Four Walls*, 129.

63 Blücher to Arendt, March 8, 1950, in ibid., 144.

64 Blücher to Arendt, July 29, 1948, in ibid., 93.

65 "Hannah Arendt and Heinrich Blücher," *Louis Proyect;* Alexander R. Bazelow, "How and Why Do We Study Philosophy: The Legacy of Heinrich Blücher" (conference, Bard College, New York, May 24, 2003); and annual letters of praise from Bard College, Hannah Arendt Papers, Library of Congress.

66 "[A]ll these people find me highly suspect," he wrote to Arendt, for example, when applying for a job at the New School. "The most restrained things I say frighten them.... Everyone has become so *clever* and respectable, and they look down on me, even though I intimidate them" (March 18, 1950, in Kohler, ed., *Within Four Walls*, 144).

67 *OT,* preface to part 3.

68 Ibid., 459.

69 Ibid., 382.

70 Ibid., 328: "This generation remembered the war [World War I] as the great prelude to the breakdown of classes and their transformation into masses."

71 David Riesman, "The Path to Total Terror," review of *The Origins of Totalitarianism* by Hannah Arendt, *Commentary*, April 1951.

72 Philip Rieff, "The Theology of Politics: Reflections on Totalitarianism as the Burden of Our Time," *Journal of Religion* 32, no. 2 (April 1952): 119–26.

73 Eric Voegelin, review of *The Origins of Totalitarianism* by Hannah Arendt, *Review of Politics,* January 1953.

74 Kazin, *New York Jew*, 196.

75 Arendt to Blücher, November 28, 1949, in Kohler, ed., *Within Four Walls*, 100.

76 Arendt to Blücher, December 14, 1949, ibid.,103.

77   *Hannah Arendt: The Last Interview,* 25.

78   Arendt to Blücher, December 14, 1949, in Kohler, ed., *Within Four Walls,* 103–4.

79   Hannah Arendt, "The Aftermath of Nazi Rule: Report from Germany," *Commentary,* October 1950.

80   Out of 565,000 in 1933: "Jewish Population of Europe in 1945," Holocaust Encyclopedia, last updated June 20, 2014, http://www.ushmm .org/wlc/en/article.php?ModuleId=10005687.

81   Arendt, "The Aftermath of Nazi Rule," 342, 344.

82   Arendt to Blücher, December 14, 1949, in Kohler, ed., *Within Four Walls,* 103.

83   Arendt to Blücher, January 3, 1950, in ibid., 114.

84   Ludz, ed., *Letters,* 57–60.

85   Arendt to Heidegger, February 9, 1950, in ibid., 59.

86   Ibid., 61.

87   Ibid., 62.

88   Arendt to Blücher, February 8, 1950, in Kohler, ed., *Within Four Walls,* 128.

89   *OT,* 326.

90   Safranski, *Martin Heidegger,* 338, 373.

91   Ibid., 373.

92   Arendt to Jaspers, August 4, 1949, in Kohler and Saner, eds., *Correspondence,* 142.

93   Hannah Arendt, "Heidegger the Fox," in *Essays in Understanding,* ed. Jerome Kohn (New York: Harcourt, Brace & Co., 1994).

94   "The Shadows," in Ludz, ed., *Letters,* 15.

95   Arendt to Heidegger, February 9, 1950, in Ludz, ed., *Letters,* 58 (Ludz translates "faraway" as "abroad"); Friedrich Schiller, "The Maiden from Afar," in *Poems of the Third Period,* available at http://www.gutenberg .org/files/6796/6796-h/6796-h.htm.

96   Heidegger to Arendt, February 1950, in Ludz, ed., *Letters,* 63.

97   Hannah Arendt, *The Human Condition* (Chicago: University of Chicago Press, 1958), 237.

98   "Forgiving, in other words, is the only reaction which does not merely re-act but acts anew and unexpectedly, unconditioned by the act which

provoked it and therefore freeing from its consequences both the one who forgives and the one who is forgiven" (ibid., 241).

99 Arendt to Jaspers, November 1, 1961, in Kohler and Saner, eds., *Correspondence*, 457.

100 Arendt, *Men in Dark Times*, 5.

101 McCarthy, "Saying Good-Bye to Hannah," *New York Review of Books*, January 22, 1976.

102 Peter Stern and Jean Yarbrough, "Teaching: Hannah Arendt," *American Scholar* 47, no. 3 (Summer 1978): 371–81.

103 Kohler, quoted in Laskin, *Partisans*, 219.

104 Arendt, "The Ex-Communists," in Kohn, ed., *Essays in Understanding*.

6: After Eichmann

1 "Thinking and Moral Considerations," *Social Research* 38, no. 3, Autumn 1973, 443.

2 Michael Denneny, interview, March 9, 2013.

3 Bellow to Arendt, December 1, 1970, in Benjamin Taylor, ed., *Saul Bellow: Letters* (New York: Viking, 2010).

4 Hannah Arendt, "A Reply to Critics," *Dissent*, Spring 1959.

5 Arendt, *The Human Condition*, 247.

6 Arendt, "Martin Heidegger at Eighty."

7 Hannah Arendt, *The Life of the Mind* (New York: Harcourt Brace Jovanovich, 1978), 19–22.

8 Hannah Arendt, "Truth and Politics," *The New Yorker*, February 25, 1967.

9 Hannah Arendt, "The Crisis in Culture: Its Social and Its Political Significance," *Between Past and Future* (New York: Viking Press, 1968), 220.

10 Hannah Arendt, "Thinking and Moral Considerations," 417–46.

11 Arendt, "The Crisis in Culture," 220.

12 Arendt, "Truth and Politics."

13 Jerome Kohn to Elisabeth Young-Bruehl, August 3, 1999, in "What and How We Learned from Hannah Arendt: An Exchange of Letters," in Mordechai Gordon, ed., *Hannah Arendt and Education: Renewing Our Common World* (Boulder, CO: Westview Press, 2001), 225–57.

14 Michael Denneny, interview, March 9, 2013.

15   Stern and Yarbrough, "Teaching: Hannah Arendt."

16   W. H. Auden, "Thinking What We Are Doing," written for the Mid-Century Book Clubs and reprinted in Arthur Krystal, ed., *A Company of Readers* (New York: Free Press, 2001).

17   McCarthy to Arendt, December 1, 1970, Brightman, ed., *Between Friends,* 272.

18   Arendt to McCarthy, September 30, 1973, ibid., 343.

19   Jaspers to Arendt, October 22, 1963, in Kohler and Saner, eds., *Correspondence,* 525.

20   Arendt, *Men in Dark Times,* 76.

21   Arendt to McCarthy, September 16, 1963, in Brightman, ed., *Between Friends,* 145.

22   Bazelow, "How and Why Do We Study Philosophy."

23   Editor's note in Brightman, ed., *Between Friends,* 266.

24   Arendt to Heidegger, November 27, 1970, in Ludz, ed., *Letters,* 173.

25   Arendt to Jaspers, April 18, 1966, in Kohler and Saner, eds., *Correspondence,* 632.

26   Edna Brocke, interview, April 18, 2013.

27   Arendt to McCarthy, December 21, 1968, cited in Young-Bruehl, *Hannah Arendt,* 533, note 37.

28   Edna Brocke, interview, April 18, 2013.

29   Arendt to McCarthy, August 22, 1975, Brightman, ed., *Between Friends,* 385–86.

30   Young-Bruehl, *Hannah Arendt,* 468.

31   David Bird, "Hannah Arendt's Funeral Held; Many Moving Tributes Paid," *New York Times,* December 9, 1975.

32   Hans Jonas, "Words Spoken at the Funeral Service of Hannah Arendt," Glenn Horowitz Archive of Rare Books and Papers.

33   Robert Lowell, "On Hannah Arendt," *New York Review of Books,* May 13, 1976.

34   Mary McCarthy, "Saying Good-Bye to Hannah."

35   Arendt, *Men in Dark Times,* 251.